THE HIGH STRANGENESS OF BIGFOOT

RONALD C. MEYER

MARK REEDER

HANGAR 1 PUBLISHING

CONTENTS

A NOTE TO OUR READERS

This book unfolds in two interwoven streams. Chapters 1, 6, 8, 10, 12, and 14 trace the chronological arc of our six-year investigation—the boots-on-the-ground reality of fieldwork, the evolution of our research protocols, and the increasingly strange phenomena we encountered while documenting what would become our film. These chapters form a continuous narrative thread you can follow from first footfall to final revelation.

The remaining chapters—2 through 5, 7, 9, 11, and 13—step back from the immediacy of field experience to explore the deeper currents flowing beneath these encounters. The documentary's timeframe simply couldn't accommodate the historical precedents, theoretical frameworks, and cross-cultural patterns necessary to understand why Bigfoot phenomena resist conventional explanation. These "phenomenon chapters" provide the expanded context—connecting our observations to larger questions about consciousness, communication, and the nature of intelligence itself—that the film's pacing had to leave behind.

You might choose to read the investigation chapters first as a complete narrative, then return to explore the conceptual landscape they traverse. Or you might prefer to move through both streams as presented, letting field experience and theoretical reflection inform each other chapter by chapter. Either path will lead you through the same essential mystery—one that deepened with each step we took into the woods, and with each new framework we discovered for understanding what we found there.

PREFACE

In 2015, filmmaker Ron Meyer was contracted by Mill Creek Entertainment to produce *Chasing Bigfoot*, a five-part investigative series examining North America's most persistent cryptozoological mystery. During the course of dozens of interviews with Bigfoot experiencers, Meyer became convinced of something fundamental: these people were describing real events. None appeared to be fabricating their accounts. Yet no one could produce the physical evidence such encounters should yield.

Then one investigator proposed something Meyer had never seriously considered: What if Bigfoot was interdimensional? At the time, the hypothesis was widely ridiculed within cryptozoological circles. For Meyer, it became an obsession.

That obsession initiated a collaboration with Bigfoot investigators Alan and Anna Megargle that would span nearly a decade, producing multiple documentary films, television series, and three books co-authored with researcher Mark Reeder. Across these works, a pattern emerged that conventional cryptozoology could not explain. A significant percentage of Bigfoot encounters exhibited characteristics fundamentally inconsistent with biological entities: instantaneous appearances and disappearances, vocalizations resembling proto-linguistic structures, physical evidence violating known biomechanics, and experiential consistencies reported by independent witnesses separated by decades and thousands of miles.

Something was responding to human attention. But it was not behaving like an animal.

The documentary, *The High Strangeness of Bigfoot*, and this companion book present a hypothesis derived substantially from ufologist and computer scientist Jacques Vallée's controversial Control System hypothesis. Vallée proposes that an ancient non-human intelligence has been guiding humanity since the emergence of language by keeping the mystery of existence ever-present—never allowing final answers, always maintaining the questions that drive humanity forward. What manifests today as Bigfoot may be one contemporary form through which this intelligence operates, adapted to modern cultural frameworks just as it once manifested through mythology, religious experience, and folklore. If this hypothesis withstands scrutiny, its implications reach far beyond cryptozoology into questions of human origins, consciousness evolution, and the fundamental nature of reality itself.

Documented in these pages, Meyer and his team's investigation does not claim definitive answers. It presents data, patterns, and a theoretical framework within which those patterns become coherent. The mystery of Bigfoot, properly understood, may be inseparable from the larger mystery of what it means to be human.

INTRODUCTION

THE THRESHOLD OF THE IMPROBABLE

What if Bigfoot isn't just hiding in the forest—what if it's hiding between realities?

This book follows filmmaker Ron Meyer and his investigation team as they set out to document Bigfoot... and discovered something far stranger. What began as a hunt for an elusive creature turned into an encounter with impossible coincidences, perfectly timed vocalizations, and phenomena that seemed to respond to the team's presence with eerie intelligence.

Again and again, they asked themselves: What if something is answering us back?

The improbable moments began to connect. A vocalization synced with meditation. Lights appearing exactly when emotions peaked. Sounds that mimicked the team's own calls with uncanny precision. It was as if reality itself was bending at the edges, revealing glimpses of a hidden intelligence that watches, waits, and interacts.

The team captured something on film that changed everything. Vocalizations that answered their calls. Audio recordings of sounds that shouldn't exist. Equipment anomalies that defied explanation. Night after night, the evidence mounted: Bigfoot wasn't just a creature hiding in the woods—it was something far more mysterious, something that seemed to exist at the very edge of our reality.

Join Ron Meyer and his team of investigators as they venture into the wilderness of Oklahoma, the dense forests of Colorado, and the high reaches of Mount Shasta at the liminal edges of civilization where the known world frays. What they found challenged everything they thought they knew about reality itself. Drawing on the groundbreaking theories of renowned scientist Jacques Vallée—who proposed that UAPs and paranormal phenomena are part of a vast 'Control System' guiding human consciousness—the team began to wonder: What if Bigfoot isn't meant to be caught... but engaged?

This is their story. An adventure into the improbable. A journey to the threshold where mystery lives.

Are you ready to step through?

1

———

HOW IT BEGAN

The road to presenting a new understanding of the odd nature of Bigfoot began when Mill Creek Entertainment asked filmmaker Ron Meyer to produce a movie on near death experiences. In the documentary *You Are Immortal*, Ron spoke with experts and ordinary people who'd had near-death experiences. The major takeaways were striking: Almost all experienced leaving the physical body. In the nonphysical world, some encountered extraordinary beings, ancestors, a vast understanding of everything, the source that some called God, and most commonly, unconditional love. Most importantly, everyone came away knowing they were immortal and had no fear of death.

Figure 1: Dr. Greer shows Alan Megargle where she had a Bigfoot encounter

During one particular interview, Rey Hernandez, director at the Consciousness and Contact Research Institute (CCRI), mentioned a person who had two near-death experiences but also contact experiences with UAPs and Bigfoot. This chance reference led to a conversation with medical doctor Melinda Greer to discuss her stories of NDEs. As a result of the conversation, it was agreed that the team—Ron Meyer, Alan Megargle, and cameraman Paul Lee—would meet with Dr. Greer in Oklahoma and film the places where she saw UAPs and had contact experiences with Bigfoot as well as another form of nonhuman intelligence.

Figure 2: Aerial view of Long Lake Resort

Each night, the team returned to Long Lake Resort near Poteau, Oklahoma—a location that turned out to be a place of high strangeness. The vacation spot is located along the banks of two privately owned lakes, Long Lake and Terrell Lake.

Lodging at the resort includes several options. There are cozy Couples Cabins, Two-Bedroom Cabins for families or groups, and Lakeside Suites that offer beautiful views and easy access to the water. The property is heavily wooded with many large deciduous trees. In addition, a small herd of buffalo roams a fenced off region of the grounds.

On the second evening of filming at the resort in 2024, Ron proposed holding a consciousness opening session to see if they could contact Bigfoot. They chose a site near one of the cabins, where a large fire pit had been made. Surrounded by tall deciduous trees, the site held an aura of expectancy. Ron decided to try something he had used before. As darkness fell, casting an awe-inspiring veil over the resort, the group eagerly sat around the rain-soaked fire pit. The air was thick with anticipation, each person feeling on the brink of something extraordinary, as if this place held a secret waiting to reveal itself.

Figure 3:Bigfoot Investigative team sitting around the firepit

Ron asked the guests to join in a simple mindfulness meditation practice.[1] He had used this mindfulness meditation in preparation for 'flow practice', based on simple martial arts interactions. This protocol had been developed in conjunction with Mark Reeder and Dmitriy Rozin, two longtime Aikido practitioners. What the three discovered was a joint unified consciousness among multiple people that allowed

---

1. Mindfulness meditation is a practice of training your mind to focus on the present moment without judgment, by paying attention to your thoughts, feelings, and sensations. It involves methods like deep breathing and body awareness to help reduce stress and improve focus. The practice is not about emptying your mind, but acknowledging and accepting whatever arises without getting carried away by it.

the participants to let go of their ego and their 'doing self' and enter a state of continuous synergetic flow with reality—hence the name 'flow state'.

Perhaps because the mindfulness meditation was so successful, Ron decided to follow the meditation with an unusual technique known as the A-E-I-O-U chant.[2] These five vowels form the basis of all verbal human communication.

After the meditation and chant protocol, the group experienced interesting interactions, including a strong sense of something present. Then, suddenly, as Dr. Greer was telling a story about the indigenous people of the area, the REM-Pod chimed, and a Presence was detected. Alan excitedly engaged with the presence, and Dr. Greer followed his lead.

In addition, when reviewing the film later, a woman's voice no one had heard during the meditation and chant could be clearly heard saying, "This is freaking me out."

During the last night at the resort, with all the filming completed, the group performed one more meditation and chant protocol around the fire pit. This time, drawn into a deeper sense of oneness with each other and nature, a mind-shattering event happened. Something heavy crashed through the treetops parallel to the ground and then landed in front of Alan and Dr. Greer with a huge ground-shaking thump.

The memory unfolded as a single moment, but around the table the details returned in slightly different ways.

Ron began. "For me it started in the trees. There was a loud crashing sound moving through the canopy—from the camp toward the car. It wasn't something dropping straight down. It had lateral motion, like it was traveling with direction. But I never heard an impact."

Paul leaned in. "That's where it's different for me. I had my back turned, reaching for the cabin door. I didn't hear the movement over-head—but I heard the landing. One dense, heavy thump. It scared me.

---

2. See Chapter 2, AEIOU, which examines the chant's origins and nature and how Meyer came across it.

It had been raining all day and my first thought was that someone had slipped and fallen hard."

Ron looked at him. "You didn't hear anything in the trees at all?"

Paul shook his head. "No. Just the thump."

Figure 4: AI rendition of a heavy object crashing through the trees

Figure 5: Paul Lee, Ron Meyer, Dr. Greer, and Alan Megargle discussing the crashing heavy object event

Dr. Greer spoke next. "I heard both. I was walking toward the car with Alan to my left. I heard something moving up in the trees, and I remember looking up, expecting to see something big coming down—a large animal or a heavy limb. It felt close, like it was going to land right near us."

Alan nodded. "Same here. I could hear it pushing through branches, then it hit the ground about six feet in front of me. I didn't just hear it—I felt it. The ground moved."

Paul frowned. "You actually felt the ground move?"

Alan nodded again. "Yeah. And remember, none of us had lights on. It was pitch black—overcast, no stars."

Paul gestured with his hands as he remembered. "I veered over and turned my headlamp on, fully expecting to see something substantial right there."

"A limb," Ron said. "An animal."

"Anything," Alan added.

Dr. Greer let out a quiet breath. "But there was nothing."

"No object," Alan said. "No fallen branch. No disturbance."

Paul sat back. "Just empty ground."

The next morning, when the team searched for the object, they found nothing.

For Dr. Greer and Alan, the crash only confirmed what they already felt—that Bigfoot had been close and somehow involved.

For Ron, it had the opposite effect. Instead of clarity, it left him with the sense that the answer to whatever Bigfoot is had slipped even farther away.

2

WHAT IS BIGFOOT?

The documentary *The High Strangeness of Bigfoot* begins with a simple question: What is Bigfoot?

Most people don't realize that the word 'Bigfoot' didn't become part of popular culture until the late 1950s and early 1960s. But that's not to say encounters with something like Bigfoot didn't happen before then. In fact, reports of large, hairy, human-like beings appear throughout history.

Long before European settlers arrived, Indigenous cultures across North America told stories of powerful, mysterious beings living in the deep forests and mountains. The word 'Sasquatch'—meaning *hairy giant*—comes from the early oral traditions of the Pacific Northwest Indigenous peoples. Across the desert southwest and throughout the rest of the country, petroglyphs, legends, and sacred stories all point to a long history of interactions between Indigenous Americans and beings remarkably similar to what we now call Bigfoot.

The first recorded encounter by a European-descended explorer occurred in 1811 near Jasper, Alberta, when a trader named David Thompson documented enormous tracks in the snow—each footprint measuring roughly fourteen inches long and eight inches wide.

At the same time, similar stories appeared around the globe. The Yeti of the Himalayas, the Yeren of China, and the Yowie of Australia all describe large, bipedal creatures that mirror the characteristics of North America's Bigfoot.

Taken together, these global parallels point to something profound: the Bigfoot phenomenon may be connected to a mystery older than recorded history—something woven into the human story itself.

Figure 6: Petroglyph of Bigfoot holding a deer, with a Bigfoot print below right

As researchers, storytellers, and scientists compared reports across cultures and time, new theories emerged to explain how such a phenomenon could exist.

One of the most influential came from an unusual collaboration between the Swiss psychologist Carl Jung and the Austrian physicist Wolfgang Pauli. Together, they explored the idea that both the physical and inner worlds of the mind might be connected by deep symbolic structures they called archetypes. Among these archetypes, one stands out: the Wild Man.

This figure appears again and again in world mythology and folk-lore, and his traits echo what we now describe as Bigfoot: strength, mystery, wilderness, and ancient wisdom. The Wild Man is not simply a monster or primitive being. He is a symbolic doorway.

In Jung's view, encountering this archetype is not merely about fear or curiosity. It represents a confrontation with our deepest instinctual nature—the part of us untouched by civilization. The Wild Man embodies freedom, raw emotion, and connection to the natural world. He mirrors the tension between who society expects us to be and who we might truly be beneath layers of culture and conditioning.

Jung believed that acknowledging and integrating this archetype leads to personal growth and even transformation, inviting authenticity, wholeness, and balance.

Figure 7: Gilgamesh from the Louvre

But there is more to this story.

Across cultures, the Wild Man is not merely a psychological symbol. Authors like Joseph Campbell, professor and scholar in comparative mythology and religion, noted that the Wild Man represents something sacred—an ancient presence deeply tied to humanity's relationship with the natural and spiritual world. In many traditions, these beings are described not just as wild creatures, but guardians of the boundary between worlds ... between nature and civilization ... between the seen and the unseen.

With that perspective, Bigfoot may not be a mere biological puzzle. Instead, the phenomenon may represent the modern expression of a pattern far older than recorded history —a guardian, a messenger, or perhaps a gatekeeper to a realm of knowledge humanity once knew... and may still be trying to remember.

The first known version of this Wild Man archetype appears in ancient Sumerian poetry from the Third Dynasty of Ur around 2100 BCE. In *The Epic of Gilgamesh*, the

Figure 8: Enkidu

gods create Enkidu—a wild, untamed being—to challenge the semi-divine king Gilgamesh. After a fierce wrestling match, the two become inseparable companions. Their adventures, including the defeat of Humbaba and the Bull of Heaven, intertwine the human world with something primal and otherworldly. When Enkidu dies, Gilgamesh is devastated, and his grief sends him on a spiritual quest for meaning, mortality, and the purpose of life. The story positions the Wild Man not merely as a beast, but as a catalyst for human transformation.

Figure 9: Attic red-figure plate from Vulci, Etruria, dated c.520-500 BC, showing an ithyphallic satyr holding an aulos, a kind of ancient Greek woodwind instrument.

This pattern continues across civilizations. In ancient Greece, the figure appears as the satyr[1] and the faun—half-human beings intimately connected to wilderness and instinct. The Romans knew a similar presence as Silvanus, the god who watched over the woods. In the Hebrew tradition, the Book of Genesis, Chapter 32 describes Jacob wrestling through the night with a mysterious being until he is blessed and renamed Israel—an encounter that mirrors the archetypal struggle between humanity and the wild, unseen forces shaping destiny.

Figure 10: In the City Art Gallery in Bradford. The figures of fauns have been attributed to Pietro Paolo Bonzi (c.1575-1636)

Throughout medieval Europe, images of the Wild Man, or Wodewose, adorned tapestries, cathedrals, shields, and carvings. Later, during the Renaissance, artists such as Martin Schongauer and Albrecht Dürer created detailed engravings depicting wild men, wild women, and even wild families—suggesting that this archetype lived deeply in the collective imagination.

---

1. According to the British classical scholar M. L. West, satyrs bear similarities to figures in other Indo-European mythologies, such as the Slavic forest deity, Leshy.

The same pattern appears worldwide. In the Himalayas, people speak of the Yeti. In Australia, Aboriginal traditions tell stories of the Yowie. Across Africa, beings such as the Koolokamba, Otang, and Waterbobbejan are described as large, humanlike, and covered in hair. South American legends include creatures like the Chimporilla, the fearsome Mapinguari with its stomach-mouth and single eye, and the Ucumar of the Andes, a shorter but powerful mountain-dwelling figure. Though these names differ, the descriptions—and the emotional responses they evoke—remain strikingly familiar.

Figure 11: Late 15th century tapestry from Basel, showing a Wodewose being tamed by a virtuous lady

In North America, the most beloved expression of this archetype is Sasquatch. Rooted in the ancestral knowledge and oral traditions of the Salish peoples of the Pacific Northwest, Sasquatch is not seen as a monster. Instead, he is regarded as a spirit-being, a teacher, or a protector—one connected to the natural world and mysteries humans have not yet fully understood. In other Native American traditions,

Sasquatch, and figures similar to it, are interpreted as guardians, messengers and gatekeepers to a realm of ancient knowledge.

Figure 12:Wild men support coats of arms in the side panels of a portrait by Albrecht Dürer, 1499 (Alte Pinakothek, Munich)

Then everything about Bigfoot changed when the Patterson-Gimlin film was released.

Filmmaker Roger Patterson and wilderness guide Bob Gimlin shot the first footage of a Bigfoot ever recorded.

Before that moment, for the general public, the creature lived mostly in folklore, newspaper curiosities, and scattered wilderness reports. But when that short, handheld sequence of a massive, upright, hair-covered being moving through Bluff Creek appeared on screens, something shifted. The mystery suddenly had anatomy, mass, motion —and a face that turned toward the camera as if acknowledging the witness behind it. It was no longer just a story. It was possible evidence that Bigfoot existed.

Figure 13: Patterson-Gimlin Bigfoot Picture

The film was captured on October 20, 1967, deep in the rugged forests of Northern California. The public first began seeing it later that same year and into early 1968 through private screenings, scientific meetings, and eventually commercial showings. And even now, more than half a century later, those sixty seconds continue to be analyzed frame by frame—stabilized, magnified, slowed, and digitally enhanced —in search of Bigfoot's reality.

Within the 8mm footage, researchers point to details that resist easy dismissal: the natural, non-mechanical gait; the visible muscle movement beneath the hair; the unusual limb proportions; and the now-iconic mid-stride turn where the creature briefly locks eyes with Bob Gimlin.

Skeptics declared hoax. Believers called it revelation. But regardless of the debate, the Patterson-Gimlin film became a dividing line. After it, sightings surged, field research expanded, and Bigfoot entered modern culture not as myth—but as a mysterious possibility.

Figure 14: Bob Gimlin with cowboy hat at conference

Both Ron Meyer and Alan Megargle have spent time speaking directly with Bob Gimlin. They describe him as a gentle, soft-spoken cowboy—honest, grounded, and visibly uncomfortable with the years of controversy and attention the film has brought him. Their conversations left a clear impression: if the Patterson-Gimlin footage were a hoax, Bob had no role in creating it.

Gimlin explained that the encounter was not staged or anticipated. He and Roger Patterson were already deep in the wilderness, riding on horseback through some of the most unforgiving terrain in Northern California. Bob wasn't a filmmaker—he was the horseman and the guide, the one who knew how to survive in that country. They were searching for something that *might* be Bigfoot, following tracks and reports, never expecting to actually see anything. According to Bob, everything changed when the creature appeared. Patterson jumped off his horse, camera in hand, while Gimlin stayed mounted, rifle ready, keeping distance and watching. "I pointed the rifle at it—that's when it looked at me," he recalled.

Bob also described what happened after the film stopped rolling. A storm moved in—fast, violent, and unforgiving. The rain turned the mountain trails into mud slicks and the river crossings into hazards. Both men, and their horses, barely made it out. That experience cemented something in Bob's mind: there was no way Patterson could have arranged for a man in a suit to be waiting in that remote location —no way someone could have arrived unseen, performed the walk, and then navigated the storm and terrain without help or risk. The conditions were simply too hostile.

In one quieter exchange years later, Bob told Meyer something unexpected. He believed Ron was on the right track in exploring Bigfoot as a phenomenon that may not be entirely physical. Over time, through stories, experiences, and patterns that refused easy explanation, Bob himself had begun leaning toward the possibility that Bigfoot might occupy a space between worlds—part biological, part something else.

For Meyer, Megargle, and countless others, the legacy of the Patterson-Gimlin film is not that it solved the mystery—but that it opened a doorway. And fifty-plus years later, that doorway has never fully closed.

3

THE BIGFOOT ALIEN
CONNECTION REVEALED

Everything about Bigfoot changed when the public sector saw the Patterson-Gimlin film.

What the film did—regardless of ongoing debates—was to give the public a vivid, lasting image of how Bigfoot looked. The creature was described in numerous reports as a towering, bipedal being standing between seven and nine feet tall, covered in thick fur—reddish, sometimes brown, sometimes black, and sometimes even pale white. Witnesses noted its broad shoulders, long swinging arms, and a conical head unlike that of any known ape.

Its walk became part of the legend: slow, deliberate, almost casual —yet unmistakably powerful. The feet appeared to land flat and evenly with each step, reinforcing the now-iconic name Bigfoot. At the same time, a picture began to form of how the creature lived.

Doug Hajicek, the producer of the *MonsterQuest* series, put it simply. "Bigfoot is singular—not plural. A lot of people think it's just one creature wandering around. But we're talking about a living, breathing population—maybe North American apes, or even humans."

Bigfoot researcher Jim Myers agreed, expanding that picture. "The misconception is that there's only one. In reality, there are probably thousands of them across the country—far more than we realize."

Doug Hajicek added a startling piece of math. "People only see them where there's wood, water, and hills. But the number of sightings is far higher than what gets reported. If we get three to four hundred reports a year, and only one percent of people are willing to report what they saw—then there would have to be at least forty thousand animals roaming North America."

Figure 15: AI created image of classic Bigfoot

One of the stars of the *Finding Bigfoot* series, Cliff Barackman, described their adaptability.

"Sasquatches are probably as adaptable to their environment as humans are. Their intelligence approaches ours." He continued, "Basically, Sasquatches can live anywhere there's food, water, and cover. And a lot of sightings happen in places no one would ever expect. I've heard of Sasquatches being reddish in color, black in color, gray, coyote colored—the fur runs the gamut and so does the skin tone as well. I've heard of kind of like Caucasian type of skin tones, I've heard gray, dark black, I've heard reddish, all these things. Sasquatches have a huge genetic diversity, as would be expected of a species like that."

Over the decades following the Patterson-Gimlin film's debut, researchers speculated that Bigfoot may live in structured groups, possibly with dominant males and females who protect the troop and drive maturing males away, much like gorillas or certain primate species. Others believe males remain mostly solitary, while females travel with their young.

Researchers and cryptozoologists also debated how these beings survived, adapted, and possibly remained hidden in a modern world, suggesting a mystery deeper and older than anyone first imagined.

By the turn of the 21st century, as reports of Bigfoot encounters exploded around the globe, the race was on to discover and document this elusive primate. Large numbers of ordinary people became Bigfoot investigators. Organizations developed and huge Bigfoot conferences occurred around the country. Podcasters spoke about evidence gathered —footprints, mysterious tree structures—as well as the myriad Bigfoot experiences and interactions by everyday people. As a result of the groundbreaking feature film *The Bigfoot Alien Connection Revealed*, Ron Meyer and Alan Megargle were invited to speak at conferences and became regulars on podcasts. In addition, the two recorded many interviews with individuals, revealing for the first time their own Bigfoot encounters—some occurring when they were young—that they had never told anyone, even family members.

Ron Boles

Figure 16a: Ron Boles

"There was seven of us there. There was three guys in front of us and there was two guys behind us and there was three of us walking in a group. One guy was named Mike, the other guy was named Gene. And we just kept on walking and then not more than four or five steps after he said something about the smell. He stopped and he was looking over his right shoulder due west and he goes, 'Oh my God.' And I'm looking over there and sure enough, from where we were standing approximately 15-20 feet away behind a tree was this big, huge figure. Like I said, its back was against the west so we couldn't really make out facial features but you could make out the shoulders and the head and fuzz, you know. And he was doing this number behind that tree like that. And I was looking at that, and he was looking at that and of course Mike was and I looked behind me to make sure those two guys were behind us because I wanted to make sure it wasn't someone pulling my leg on me. No, they were back there. I looked in front of me, those guys were there too. Then I looked back and this thing was just doing this number. Gene at that point goes, 'I can't handle this' and he took off running. Being that he was the biggest one of us, I followed suit."

Marc DeWerth

Figure 16b: Marc Dewerth

"All of a sudden, I start to see this thing standing up, like going up in an upward position and I'm thinking I'm going to see ears here and a mouth or a nose and all of a sudden it turns and looks at me and when it started turning I could see this, and a flat face. I'm like, oh my God, I think this is a Bigfoot. And when you saw how big the thing was, it was like incredible and I had a camera in my pack, so I swung my bag around and when I did it turned and went right up the next tier and it was gone."

Not all accounts of Bigfoot phenomena are clear visual sightings. Some people, like Norma Parda, Patrick Ferguson, and Scott Rawlins, report loud noises such as tree breaks or something circling them.

Perhaps most curious and mysterious is that when people actually see the elusive creatures, it is often by accident.

Derek Randles

Figure 16c: Derek Randles

"The number one way to have a Sasquatch encounter, statistically, is have one cross the road in front of your vehicle. Most of the sightings that have ever been recorded happened that way. So you go out into their habitat as a human being and you go try to find one, and you're more likely to win the lottery twice before you happen to find one. They're so elusive

and there's so few of them and they're so incredibly
intelligent."

Jim Myers

Figure 16d: Jim Myers, owner of the Sasquatch Outpost

"It's funny, the people who seem to see Bigfoot the most are
not looking for Bigfoot. They're hiking, not looking for
Bigfoot and they have an encounter, a dramatic encounter that
have so rocked these people's world that they almost go into
hiding for weeks after the event because everything they
thought they knew about the world and the woods and everything, suddenly they see a creature they thought was a myth,
and it was real."

Reactions vary from shock to excitement to bland acceptance. Native
American Winona Kirk told us, "Psychologically, I was in shock." So
did Snuffy DeStefano. On the other hand, Shane Carpenter shrugged
off any feelings of fear, stating, "I wasn't scared." While Norma Prada
said, "I get excited thinking about it."

Whether these sightings are really Bigfoot—or a case of misidenti-
fication, or a mere hoax—remains controversial. But one thing is clear:

most of the witnesses are forever changed, never to live the same life again.

Interestingly, the most common physical evidence linked to Bigfoot hasn't been hair, bones, or clear photographs—it has been footprints. These impressions found in soil, mud, snow, or sand became the first clues many researchers took seriously. Early investigators began pouring plaster into these tracks to preserve them, and before long, plaster casting became a standard part of Bigfoot fieldwork.

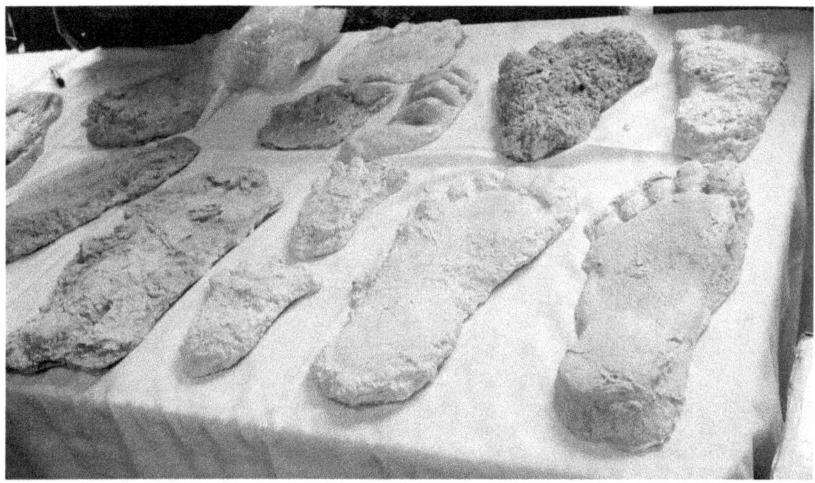

Figure 17: Bigfoot plaster casts from Cliff Barackman's collection

Today, thousands of casts exist in private collections, museums, and research archives. Some are intricate, showing dermal ridges, mid-tarsal breaks, and anatomical structure that skeptics argue would be difficult to fake. Others are crude, suspicious, and clearly created for attention or profit.

The first famous cast is often credited to Jerry Crew, a construction equipment operator working in Northern California in 1958. When Crew found massive tracks surrounding his work site, he made a cast and brought it to a local newspaper. The resulting photo—Crew holding a plaster cast and looking bewildered—became the moment the word "Bigfoot" entered modern culture.

But the story didn't end there. Over the decades, accusations of hoaxing swirled around Crew's discovery. Some claimed the prints were real but the story around them was manipulated. Others argued the casts were faked using a wooden foot-making device, yet no working version ever matched the detail found in the originals.

Figure 18: Picture of Jerry Crew with Bigfoot plaster cast

By the 1980s, the cultural tone shifted. Bigfoot became a punchline —not a mystery. Grocery-store tabloids splashed absurd headlines like "Bigfoot Steals Child; Escapes on UFO!" across their covers, and for many Americans, images of a large, brutish hairy ape became the default association with this mysterious yet heralded cryptid. This not-so-subtle form of ridicule helped push the topic underground. While the mystery never disappeared, Bigfoot became harder to take seriously.

Everything changed again at the arrival of the 21st century.

Figure 19: Bigfoot Sculpture from Remer, Minnesota, courtesy of CBS News

With the explosion of cable television and streaming platforms, Bigfoot resurfaced—not as a joke, but as a legitimate mystery worth exploring. Documentaries such as *MonsterQuest*, *Finding Bigfoot*, and eventually *Expedition Bigfoot* brought new energy to the subject. They introduced night-vision footage, audio analysis, eyewitness interviews, and field investigations—tools that made the search for Bigfoot feel scientific and important. Suddenly, Bigfoot wasn't just folklore—it became a cultural phenomenon. And like UAPs, it pushed past consensus science and ignited the imagination of millions of people.

At the same time, social media gave everyday people—campers, hunters, hikers, drone enthusiasts—a way to share sightings instantly with the world. Videos, thermal captures, trail-cam images, and strange audio recordings spread rapidly online. With that new visibility came something unexpected: the number of reported encounters began to rise dramatically.

Parallel to this growing awareness, an entire global marketing and cultural industry formed around Bigfoot. Festivals, merchandise, tourism, themed restaurants, and roadside attractions turned the creature into a cultural icon. In some regions, Bigfoot became a mascot for wilderness protection, cryptid research, and even local identity.

The small town of Remer in northern Minnesota trademarked the title "Home of Bigfoot" and now holds annual Bigfoot Days.

Derek Randles of the *Bigfoot Olympic Project* explains, "The way I look at it is there's probably five or six thousand serious researchers in the world. A lot of those researchers are pretty much armchair researchers that do their research from the computer and don't get out a whole lot. And then there's probably a smaller number that actually get out in the field and do the research hands on."

For Meyer and Megargle, everything changed during the interview with Jim Myers, owner of the Sasquatch Outpost in Bailey, Colorado. Jim explained how his ideas of Bigfoot evolved over the decades.

Jim Meyers

"When I started doing Bigfoot research, my thinking was Bigfoot is a real, flesh and blood creature, lives in the forest, must be very elusive. I don't know how they hide from people like they apparently do, but the more I've researched this, the more people I've talked to, the more experiences I've heard about where I can't say what I think, but I don't discount anything anymore. When someone comes in and says I once saw Bigfoot and it disappeared while I was watching it, or strange things that have happened, lights have bounced through the woods at night and then a Bigfoot appears or just their ability to be there, then not be there. Tracks that people are following that simply stop and there's no more track. So, I've definitely moved towards the paranormal or supernatural side of Bigfoot just because I can't explain so much of what I've read or heard."

The idea that Bigfoot might be something para-physical—or even interdimensional—led to Meyer and Megargle's groundbreaking 2017 feature documentary *The Bigfoot Alien Connection Revealed*. The film reached a massive audience, earning more than eight million views across streaming platforms. But its real impact went deeper than numbers.

For many viewers, the documentary shifted how they thought and felt about Bigfoot. Suddenly, Bigfoot was no longer confined to the realm of an elusive biological creature. The possibility of a connection to UAPs, consciousness, and the paranormal transformed the conversation. The phenomenon seemed to behave less like a hiding animal and more like something responsive—aware of human attention and intentionally elusive. This pattern echoed what researcher Jacques Vallée had long described in his Control System hypothesis: certain phenomena appear designed not to be caught, but to influence human perception and belief.

As a result, something unexpected and somewhat miraculous happened. People began to talk. Thousands came forward—some quietly, some with relief, others with awe—to share their own strange encounters. Not just sightings or footprints, but experiences that crossed the boundary between the physical world and something far stranger.

Primatologist Dr. Esteban Sarmiento described this phenomenon. "If you live long enough, you've seen things that you can't explain. And I think a lot of people have had this phenomenon, but until you have TV and the internet, everybody can't communicate about it because most of us just put it in the back of the mind and it disappears. It's almost like this event that happened maybe twice or three times, it doesn't keep happening and there's really no point in talking because most people aren't going to listen and they're not going to believe you. But then when you have other people that it happened to, then you can get together and talk about it and have a group, it's almost like alcoholics anonymous."

Among these Bigfoot reports were a growing number of people coming forward with accounts that Bigfoot was something more than physical.

Dave Kumm is a jack-of-all-trades living in eastern Nebraska. He has never told his Bigfoot story until now.

> "I am driving down this road and it's covered with trees and this big bipedal thing, it walks in front of me it doesn't look at me or nothing and crosses the road. And I'm like what is that? I'm on the reservation, so I'm like well maybe it's a big Native American guy. You know it just didn't look right. I get down to the end of the trees where I thought it was crossing and I look out the field and it was walking away from me, a dark hairy figure, and it stayed out in the open field and as it walked away then it just like faded out like it pixelated, a lot of people say like in the Predator movie. That's what I've seen."

Jim Urland, a burly Colorado contractor, tells a similar story.

> "We were walking into a clearing where I could see there were trees about 20 yards apart. And he was walking in between to crap in the pine trees. And as he walked into the clearing there was a shimmer. A shimmer began as a circle started big and got smaller. And as he kept walking they got into the center and it just went away. And at that point it was gone."

Native American Shaman Jim White tells about his encounter.

> "I was cutting wood on the Santee Dakota Indian reservation. It was early in the morning, and I looked up because I felt something staring at me, and by this 20-foot giant cedar tree I see something staring at me. I call it Bigfoot. It was shimmering, you could see through it. But you can still see the outline of it.

Even many years later he comes around usually when we're having our ceremonies."

At the same time, a growing number of sensitives[1] and psychics came forward with accounts of how they were in contact and guided by the presence of Bigfoot.

Gail Fowler a well-known Shamanic sensitive:

"Humans and Sasquatch have worked side-by-side as brothers. I keep hearing from them that they want to work with us. They want to teach us but they also want to learn from us. I've had a vision where Bigfoot comes in and sits in front of us and wants to teach us. I'm looking forward to this."

Garrett Duncan, a Navajo Shaman, is in constant contact with Bigfoot:

"I feel a Bigfoot coming in right now. He's right here and the reason I know this is I heard this click sound. It's kind of like they part this dimension and then they come through and it closes. It makes a sound like a wood knock. Energetically I can feel him standing right behind me. He's not in his dense 3D body and is able to separate himself out of that container and move quickly."

So, by the early 2020s, the Bigfoot debate had reached a turning point. For decades, the central question had been simple: Is Bigfoot a biological creature or something paranormal?

But after years of searching—without bones, bodies, or conclusive physical traces—yet with a rising number of strange sightings and experiences, the tide began to shift.

---

1. Sensitives are individuals who experience an acute awareness of non-ordinary reality, often manifesting as empathy, precognition, clairsentience, or even deep-seated fear/terror in the presence of an unknown force. See Appendix 1.

Seasoned investigators, many of whom had spent a lifetime assuming Bigfoot was flesh and blood, started rethinking their position. The nature of the evidence was changing. More encounters included sudden disappearances, glowing eyes, unusual lights, psychic impressions. At the same time, new technology was responding as if to an unseen intelligence. The phenomenon seemed less like a hidden species and more like a carefully managed mystery—one that revealed itself selectively, almost as if testing human response. This mirrored Vallée's Control System hypothesis: that anomalous phenomena might function as a conditioning mechanism, slowly reshaping collective belief systems through carefully dosed encounters.

Nick Redfern, one of the earliest veteran Bigfoot investigators to cross over told Meyer, "The ability of these creatures to elude us one hundred percent of the time. No other animal than the so-called Bigfoot are able to achieve that."

One of the most respected lifelong Bigfoot field researchers, Lyle Blackburn, explained, "As you go, of course you're exposed to other possibilities. I mean they play in all sorts of things, are they UAPs ... aliens ... extraterrestrials? Are they coming through portals ... interdimensional creatures? Do they have supernatural abilities? Are they not so much biological as a phenomenon that we don't understand?"

Even the most recognizable faces in the field—the stars of *Finding Bigfoot* and *Expedition Bigfoot*—quietly admitted they had witnessed events that didn't fit a purely biological explanation. Encounters they were never allowed to share on television.

James "Bobo" Fay from *Finding Bigfoot:*

"The whole production crew were sitting there watching these two orbs following Bigfoot along. We measured they were 70 feet from us going at a walking pace. Natives tell me when they are traveling sometimes they travel in their spirit form, it's like a ball. A ball of light. Some say they can cloak or whatever, I don't know what's going on but I'm opening to it. For sure."

Ronny LeBlanc, star of *Expedition Bigfoot:*

"We've experienced paranormal Bigfoot on the show Expedition Bigfoot. I believe we captured footage of this and what's amazing is it was edited out by the network. It was me talking to the Bigfoot saying, 'we know you're up there yourself.' And it did."

So, new possibilities about what Bigfoot is were already emerging in the zeitgeist when Meyer and Megargle had their anomalous experience in Oklahoma. Maybe Bigfoot wasn't just an undiscovered species. Maybe Bigfoot was part of a mystery far older and far stranger than anyone expected—a phenomenon that, like UAPs and other high strangeness events, seemed to operate at the threshold between the physical and something beyond.

4

TOOLS FOR FINDING BIGFOOT

During the making of the 2015 series *Chasing Bigfoot*, filmmaker Ron Meyer interviewed dozens of witnesses—hunters, hikers, and ordinary people who stumbled into something impossible. Again and again, the pattern was the same: Bigfoot encounters never happened on schedule. They happened suddenly, without warning—at the edge of campfires, on lonely trails, or crossing a remote road.

Also during the filming of *Chasing Bigfoot* when Meyer met Bigfoot investigators Alan Megargle and Jesse Morgan at a conference, he was surprised to hear about an unusual Bigfoot event. The two men told him they hosted at an unusual gathering called Bigfoot Adventure Weekends where, for three days in Ohio's Salt Fork State Park, people from across the country converged with a singular intention. Unlike typical encounters that happened by chance, the participants actively sought Bigfoot.

Meyer was intrigued. During that same conference, he arranged permission to bring his film crew—including co-producer and editor Anna Meyer-Evans—to the Bigfoot weekend. What began as a practical decision quickly became personal. Anna and Alan would later marry, and she would join Megargle and Morgan's paranormal investigation team.

It was during that weekend when Meyer witnessed something unexpected: the pursuit of Bigfoot was no longer just wandering through forests with a flashlight and hope. Investigators had developed protocols—deliberate methods meant to signal, attract, and communicate. Night ops took participants deep into the park, walking single-file down dark trails while experimenting with calls, knocks, and intentional sounds.

Back home in Colorado, Meyer realized his own documentary team needed to try these techniques firsthand.

He contacted Jim Myers, owner of the Sasquatch Outpost in Bailey, Colorado, and arranged a nighttime expedition into the wilderness near the Colorado Trail. The plan was simple: hike into a remote campsite, set up audio equipment, and attempt contact.

Figure 20: Anna Megargle, Jesse Morgan, and Alan Megargle

Jim explained the process with the calm confidence of someone who had done this many times. "We figured out pretty early we're never going to sneak up on a Bigfoot. So instead, we let them know we're here. Make noise while we walk. Knock on trees. Maybe give a whoop or two. And once we reach the spot—then we go still. Then we wait."

When the team reached the campsite, they set up a recorder to run through the night. Jim pulled out what looked like a modified baseball bat and prepared to perform a wood knock—a technique many field researchers believe acts like a primitive communication channel. A wood knock is a deep, deliberate strike: wood against wood. The sound carries through forest timber farther than the human voice ever could.

Some believe it is Bigfoot's version of language, a way of announcing territory, curiosity, or a warning.

Jim hefted the bat and hit the tree. The crack echoed across the valley. Almost immediately, before anyone could speak, another knock answered from somewhere out in the darkness.

Meyer was stunned.

Jim knocked again. This time the reply was louder, sharper, unmistakable.

Later, when the team listened to the recording, the return knocks were clear—two distinct replies from something that had answered their call.

For Meyer and his daughter Anna, this moment marked a shift. Something out there had heard them—and responded.

For the first time, the mystery of Bigfoot felt alive.

* * *

The second approach to attracting Bigfoot was based on reports by field researchers of hearing whoops or howls they felt Bigfoot had produced. As a result, investigators initiated their own whoops or howls in hopes of attracting a Bigfoot to respond or show up. Alan Megargle recalls one of the first times he experienced the call-and-response phenomenon in the field.

"On one occasion working with Jesse Morgan, he does these really loud, guttural howls, and he did it in Ohio. As the howl ended, we heard coyotes, but the very first thing that it triggered was not a coyote but something else. When we listened to the audio we recorded, there was something else that sounded like a howl that responded before the coyotes."

The third technique for inviting interaction is known among researchers as creating a gifting site. The idea is simple: leave small objects—trinkets, food, tokens—on a chosen spot and walk away. If something has changed when you return, if an object has been moved, rearranged, or replaced, then you may be standing inside a dialogue—one conducted without words.

* * *

For the conclusion of *The Bigfoot Alien Connection Revealed*, the team traveled to one of the most unusual paranormal hotspots in the Pacific Northwest—a place the well-known Bigfoot investigator Tobe Johnson named the Owl Moon Lab. Located south of Eugene, Oregon, this quiet rural property had become a crossroads where Bigfoot encounters, poltergeist-like events, strange lights, and even alien phenomena unfolded with uncanny regularity.

The Owl Moon Lab belonged to retired builder Darrell Adams and his wife, recent transplants from California who had come north to be closer to their grandchildren. Nothing about the property looked unusual—an ordinary home, a modest yard, a metal shed. Yet the shed, of all places, appeared to be the origin point for much of the activity. Tobe Johnson, who had spent countless nights documenting the phenomena, was eager to show the team the extraordinary gifting site set up just beyond it.

Tobe explained what made this site different from the typical offerings researchers leave in the woods.

Tobe Johnson

The gifts here are extremely personal. Whatever is interacting with this family isn't just listening—it seems to understand the people who live here. Objects show up out of nowhere... or from seemingly nowhere.

One day I came home from work—I was living in that little camper over by the tree line—and Darrell and I walked into the shed to download audio from the night before. When I stepped back out, something was sparkling on top of the camper roof. It was gold. I had just been looking at the camper. There was nothing there. And it's eight feet to the top—you can't just drop something up there by accident.

This happens all the time now. We turn around and things

appear. Recently, Darrell's wife joked, 'Bring us a bag of gold—bring us some gold.' So when I saw that gold up there, I thought, okay... this presence has a sense of humor. When I brought it down, I expected pyrite. But it was an old rifle casing from the 1800s.

Next, Tobe brought the crew to the gifting platform—a flat slab of rock where they arranged objects and letters. He explained, "We started spelling messages with small wooden cubes—something a lot of Bigfoot researchers do. Once, I laid out the letters to say, 'Thank you for gifts.' Three days later, we came back... and the message had been changed. Using the letters—and numbers, because we didn't have enough letters—it read: 'w3l4ome.' They used the number 3 as an E and the number 4 as a C. No normal animal could do that."

Figure 21: Tobe Johnson's wooden cubes

Across interviews, Alan Megargle kept hearing versions of the same story from Bigfoot researchers around the country: these gifting sites sometimes develop into long-term relationships. Objects come and go. Patterns change. Gifts are responded to—or rejected. Something out there is paying attention.

Looking back, Ron realized that the presence moving through these encounters wasn't simply an animal avoiding detection. Through the Bigfoot phenomenon itself, a new cultural mystery was already unfolding—one that suggested intelligence, intention, and a desire to be noticed, just enough to keep humanity wondering.

* * *

What was happening at the same time was that Bigfoot researchers had carved out what they called hotspots. These remote locations functioned as field laboratories—places where investigators returned year after year to observe patterns, document anomalies, and search for signs that something unusual had passed through. They looked for peculiar tree structures, such as bent limbs, disturbed ground, and, in rare cases, the possibility of nesting sites. Secrecy ruled everything. These hotspots were guarded like buried treasure in an Indiana Jones movie, hidden from the public and even from other investigators.

The hotspots stretched across North America and into Canada. Some were tucked deep inside national forests; others sat quietly on public land. A few researchers simply wanted the thrill of an encounter, but others kept meticulous records, hoping that long-term data might reveal patterns of behavior.

Among the most respected Bigfoot investigators is Derek Randles, co-founder of the Olympic Project in the Pacific Northwest—one of the few organizations dedicated to long-term, scientific-style documentation of Bigfoot. Derek told the film crew about the project.

Derek Randles

"The Olympic Project started as an aggressive camera-trap program. And over the last seven or eight years, it has morphed into a full study project.

We document everything. If we find a good set of tracks, we record every detail possible. And over time, if the evidence is credible, we start seeing patterns emerge. We're trying to put those patterns together with the hope that one day we can predict what the species is—and where it's going to be."

Many of these dedicated researchers eventually became familiar voices on the conference circuit as well as podcasts. They were the ones bringing Bigfoot out of the fringe and into the cultural conversation. They described feelings of being watched; small rocks tossed from the tree line; strange, almost geometric tree structures; blurry photos hinting at a figure just beyond recognition; and, of course, casts of footprints—always presented proudly, as though each plaster print were a passport stamped from another world.

Figure 22a: Bigfoot nest

For Ron Meyer and his team, one of the most revealing field investigations took place with Michael Johnson and Scott Barta of S.I.R.— Sasquatch Investigations of the Rockies. They led the crew into their secret research area deep in the southern Colorado mountains, a place marked by classic signs of Bigfoot presence and multiple reported sightings.

On the final morning of the expedition, Scott and Mike guided Ron and his daughter Anna to something extraordinary: a possible Bigfoot nest, a structure they believed could be used to shelter young Bigfoot.

Mike Johnson told them that morning, "Alright, we're here. This is the spot where I found the nest. It's a really cool piece of Bigfoot evidence."

What Ron saw was striking. The nest had been constructed with care and intention. Branches of soft balsam had been torn from trees four to five feet above the ground—clean breaks, with no claw marks. A few strands of hair lay caught in the bedding. Michael collected them carefully, and the material, along with video, was sent to researcher and filmmaker Doug Hajicek for analysis.

Figure 22b: Mike Johnson taking samples from Bigfoot nest

Under magnification, the hairs showed darker pigmentation at the bulb that tapered toward the ends. Morphologically, it suggested a large mammal like a deer—but Hajicek could not rule out the possibility of Bigfoot. It was just as plausible that the hairs belonged to prey brought to the nest.

The nest itself, however, was another matter. Hajicek called it one of the best potential Bigfoot nests he had ever examined. No known North American animal—except humans or Bigfoot—would tear branches directly from trees to build a structure like this. Other animals gather material from the ground. This was different. It showed intent.

For Ron, it became the most compelling piece of evidence he filmed for his documentary series *Chasing Bigfoot*.

Later, during the filming of *The Bigfoot Alien Connection Revealed*, two remarkable events shifted Ron and Alan's thinking about the Bigfoot phenomenon in ways they did not expect.

The first came from an ordinary rural couple in Washington State with an extraordinary story. They insisted on anonymity, but in confidence they described something crucial. On their property, they had performed a simple invitation ritual meant to call Bigfoot closer. And soon after, something answered. What arrived wasn't merely a fleeting sound or distant shape. The presence was felt, and physical interactions followed.

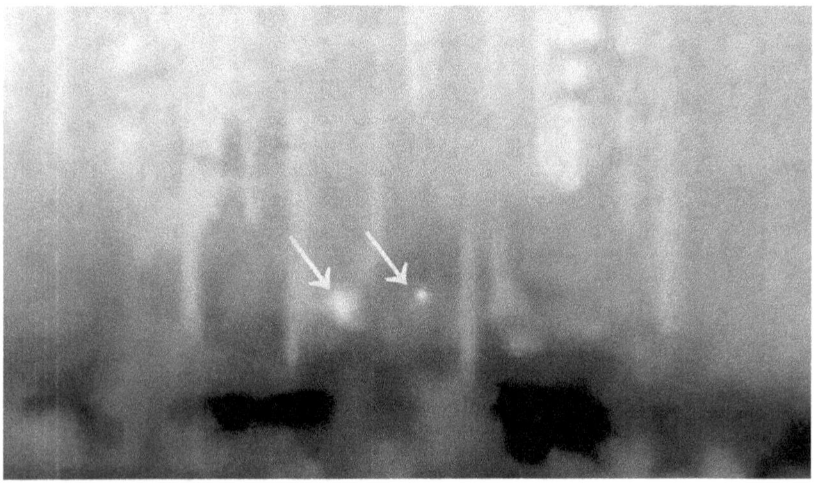

Figure 23: FLIR Heat Signature Image of two large creatures

For Ron and Alan, the implications went far beyond the ritual itself. What mattered was the underlying idea: intention appeared to matter. Consciousness might play a role in these encounters.

The second moment unfolded deep in the forests of the Olympic Peninsula when researcher Derek Randles shared a series of strange images captured on a FLIR camera—technology that senses infrared radiation and translates heat into visible imagery. Unlike a regular video camera, a FLIR unit does not record light. It reveals temperature differences, picking up the warmth of living bodies even in total darkness. Hunters use them to spot animals at night. Search-and-rescue teams use them to locate missing people.

But what Randles showed was unlike anything those fields normally encounter. On the screen, massive upright heat signatures moved among the trees—large, bipedal forms navigating the forest with deliberate intelligence. They were not elk. They were not bears. Indeed, they were far too tall and their movements far too fluid to match any known wildlife. Randles had captured something that the human eye would never have seen.

For Ron and Alan, this marked a major turning point in the entire field of Bigfoot research. Investigators were beginning to move beyond observation—documenting sightings or collecting trace evidence—and into something far more provocative: interaction with the elusive creatures. Attempts to engage and even communicate with the Bigfoot phenomenon itself.

That idea gained momentum in 2020 with the release of the television series *The Mystery of Skinwalker Ranch* on the History Channel. For the first time, a scientific team wasn't just documenting anomalies—they were probing them.

The investigators at Skinwalker Ranch deployed a wide range of advanced tools: thermal cameras to detect hotspots and cold zones that might indicate portals; FLIR systems to track moving heat signatures; specialized electromagnetic and magnetic field meters to measure spikes and distortions; laser systems, spectrum analyzers, RF equipment, LiDAR mapping, drones, and even rockets to provoke a response.

And something did respond—though not always in the manner researchers hoped.

Equipment malfunctioned precisely when experiments intensified. Magnetic field spikes appeared where nothing physical was present. Cold zones and atmospheric anomalies formed in patterns no known technology or weather system could explain. Sometimes, the experiments seemed to trigger a direct and intelligent reaction—one that was measurable.

Research was no longer mere passive observation. It had become interaction. And with each new tool deployed, the phenomenon seemed to respond in kind—calibrating itself to stay one step ahead, revealing just enough to awaken curiosity while concealing just enough to keep the mystery alive.

For Ron Meyer and Alan Megargle, the use of sophisticated scientific instrumentation changed everything. If scientists could use consciousness-infused intention and advanced sensing tools to interact with an unseen presence at Skinwalker Ranch, then perhaps the Bigfoot phenomenon—long treated as a biological mystery—could also be approached as a responsive nonhuman intelligence.

These realizations about how to interact with Bigfoot became the foundation of their next documentary: *Alien Contact in the Rockies*. It was a bold challenge to see whether technology, awareness, and intention could open a window into the mystery of Bigfoot.

The investigation started with an experiment they conducted on a forty-acre property near Rocky Mountain National Park, one of the centers of Bigfoot activity in Colorado, that had been in the Meyer family since the 1980s.

The parcel of land lay on the fringe of true wilderness—an untouched slice of the broader Rocky Mountain ecosystem, where bears, elk, moose, mountain lions and, according to many, Bigfoot still roam. From the start, the property radiated a subtle strangeness. Along the Little Thompson River, Ron and Alan discovered bone piles—cleaned, deftly arranged in particular designs and, in several cases, missing skulls. Bones would echo throughout the investigation in increasingly uncanny ways. In human mythology, bones are the sacred, enduring scaffolding of existence, representing the unyielding core of ancestry, the potential for ultimate renewal, and the profound, tangible link between mortality and rebirth. They are also used in casting fortunes. Bone divination is part of an ancient practice of casting various objects—bones, stones, shells, keys, charms—onto a surface to read patterns for guidance, insight, or predicting the future.

Whenever the team visited the land, Alan opened the session with a deerskin drum—crafted by a Pacific Northwest Native American from the hide of a deer infused with possible Bigfoot hairs. For Alan, the drum wasn't ceremonial; it was a communicative ritual. Every resonant beat was an intentional signal to the unseen world: We're here. We're listening. We want to interact.

Figure 24: Alan Megargle holding up the empty bottle

After a spring snowstorm, Ron, Alan, and Anna found a trail of wide, humanlike prints near a bone bed. The tracks extended only a short distance before abruptly ending—classic para-physical behavior reported in Bigfoot encounters. Backtracking them was equally bizarre: the prints vanished at an anthill with no indication of approach or departure. As a result, they laid out multiple gifting sites across the property.

For months, there was no response at any of the gifting sites. The silence became part of the landscape—quiet, still, and almost dismissive. But then, at one of their most remote gifting sites, something happened that changed everything.

Ron and Alan had placed a small bottle into a deep rock crevice, sealing a single feather inside. The crevice was tight, the location steep and isolated, accessible only by scrambling over private land few others ever set foot on. The bottle itself was untouched—no scratches or signs of tampering. But the feather was gone.

Figure 25: Alan Megargle and Kenny Collins inspecting the deer mutilation

A few feet away, they found the feather inserted inside a narrow crack in a nearby boulder, slipped into a fissure so thin it would have required precision and dexterity. No hiker could have found it. No wind could have lifted it. No animal could have removed it from the bottle, carried it intact, and placed it so carefully.

The message was unmistakable: something had interacted with their offering and placed it where they would find it.

It was a classic gifting-site response—intelligent, personal, and intentional—and it occurred at the exact spot where the most extraordinary events would soon unfold.

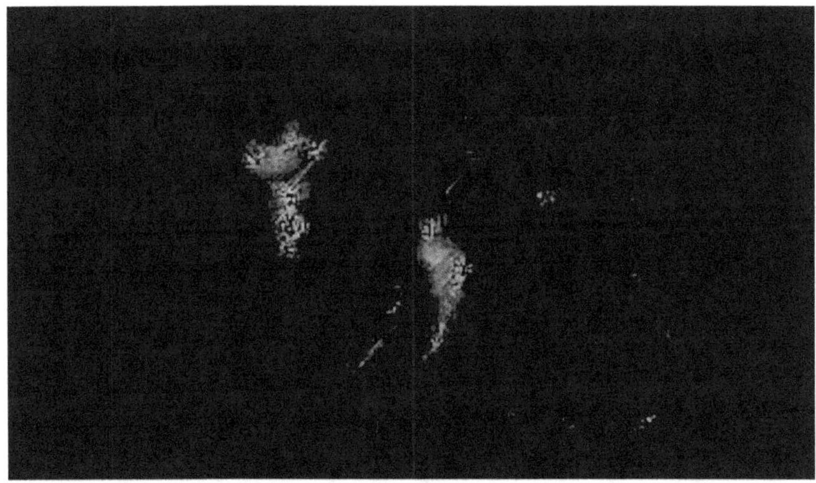

Figure 26a: Strange brontosaurus-like creature

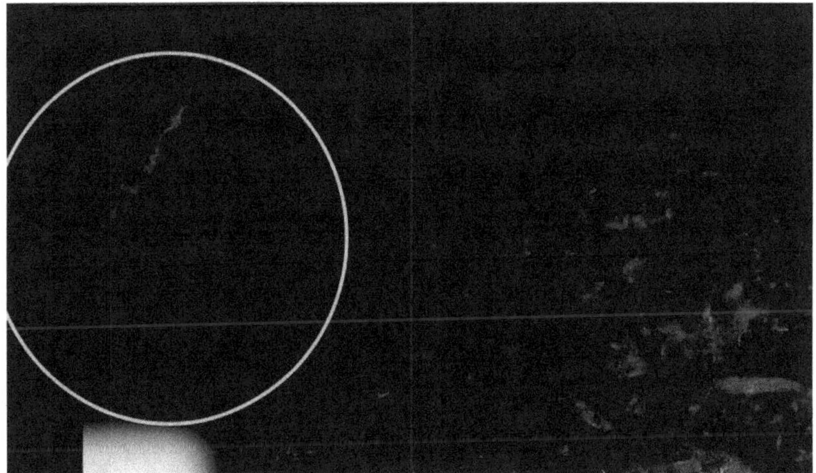

Figure 26b: Strange creature

But as unusual and profound as this interaction had been, nothing prepared them for what appeared after the next round of winter storms.

At the base of a rugged rock formation—directly below the gifting site—they found a freshly mutilated deer. The remains had been placed deliberately, almost ceremonially. No tracks led to them. No blood surrounded the deer. It had not been dragged, hunted, or scavenged. The carcass had simply appeared.

The scene echoed the long, unsettling history of animal mutilations across the West: deer, cattle, horses, sheep. Clean cuts. Tissue missing. The complete absence of struggle.

Ron and Alan had brought a TriField EMF Meter—a device that measures fluctuations in magnetic fields and radio-frequency energy.[1]

As Alan circled the deer carcass with the meter, strong magnetic field readings fluctuated in intensity, rising and falling in distinct patterns. When the data was mapped, the spikes outlined a kind of invisible dome above the carcass and gifting site—an area of distortion unlike anything produced by natural geology or man-made equipment.

The carcass showed bones that were both snapped and clean-cut—a combination common in high-strangeness mutilation cases.

To monitor the area, they set up a trail cam, recording what occurred around the mutilated deer.

Over the following weeks, the camera captured normal wildlife—a fox slipping through the shadows, a bobcat stalking past, magpies hopping around the carcass. The images were crisp, proof the equipment was fully functional, both day and night. Then one night, surprising frames of static occurred. The camera recorded sudden bursts of interference forming the same dome shape reflected in the earlier magnetic readings.

Then the impossible arrived. The trail cam recorded a small brontosaurus-like creature, flickering in and out of the frame as if struggling to remain corporeal. Its long neck moved as if looking around to see where it was. Days later, after the camera was remounted, a second entity appeared: a mythic hybrid of cat and dog, crouched low as it moved across the frame, its body rippling in and out of existence. Neither creature resembled any known animal on the planet.

Heavy storms delayed further visits. When the team finally

---

1. In physics, electric fields, magnetic fields, and electromagnetic radiation are intimately connected. A changing electric field generates a magnetic field, and vice versa. Together they form the basis of electromagnetic waves—from the lowest radio frequencies to visible light and beyond. These fields govern how energy moves through space and interact with matter, and disturbances in them can signal the presence of unseen forces or structures.

returned, the carcass had almost completely vanished—and so had the magnetic field.

As they descended from the site, Ron noticed something resting neatly on the moss-covered forest floor: a perfectly preserved lower deer leg bone, placed with intention, like a final signature on a message they were only beginning to understand. A message with many questions.

Had they opened a portal?

Had something acknowledged their ritual drumming?

Or had they simply stumbled into a phenomenon already in motion —a presence subtly guiding them deeper into the ways of the Bigfoot mystery?

Whatever the truth, one thing was undeniable: something intelligent, intentional, and profoundly strange had been present.

The team's work on the mystery of the Bigfoot phenomenon did not end with this one profound encounter. Beginning in the fall of 2022 and extending into the spring of 2023, the team engaged in a ten-day investigation of Bradshaw Ranch near Sedona, Arizona. What they encountered there would become one of the most revealing chapters in their exploration of high strangeness, resulting in a highly successful documentary feature, *The Mysteries of Bradshaw Ranch: Aliens, Portals and the Paranormal*, and a companion book, *The High Strangeness of Bradshaw Ranch*.

Beginning in the 1990s, Bradshaw Ranch emerged as one of the most complete and perplexing paranormal hotspots in North America —second only to Skinwalker Ranch in terms of the sheer range, intensity, and consistency of anomalous phenomena reported. Unlike most sites that specialize in one type of mystery, Bradshaw Ranch was a convergence zone. Witnesses reported everything from craft-like lights skimming the mesas to shadowy figures moving through the junipers, sudden temperature drops, time distortions, inexplicable footprints, poltergeist-like activity inside abandoned structures, and even moments where the landscape itself seemed to shift—as if two worlds overlapped for a breath and then snapped apart again.

For decades, stories circulated of portal zones on the property, places where researchers and locals alike observed luminous spheres drifting silently through the air before vanishing as though slipping between dimensions. Former owner Linda Bradshaw documented encounters with entities she described as partially physical—appearing solid one moment and ghostlike the next.

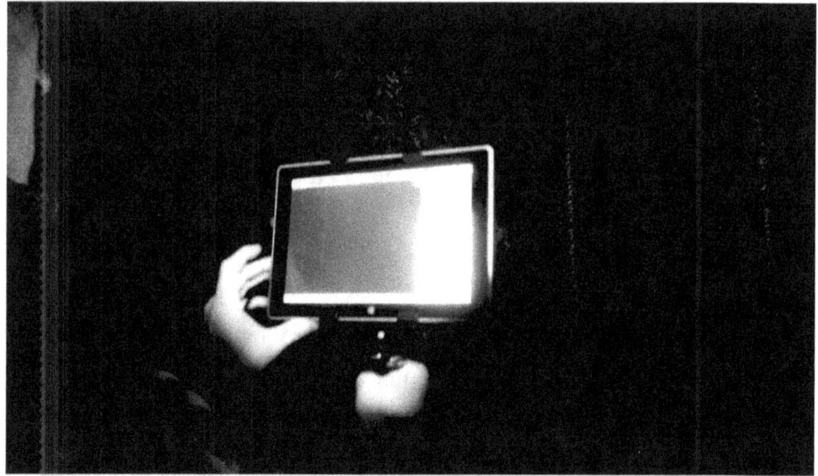

Figure 27: SLS Kinect camera

By the time the team arrived in 2022, the ranch had already gained a near-mythic status. It was a crossroads of mysteries: UAPs, interdimensional anomalies, cryptid encounters, and a persistent intelligence that seemed to respond to human presence. The site had been closed to the public for years, now under federal control for reasons that have never fully been explained.

At Bradshaw Ranch, Alan and Ron expanded their paranormal and Bigfoot technological toolkit with several devices originally developed for ghost-hunting research—technologies designed to detect and energize the mysterious presence into interaction with them. They brought in an SLS Kinect camera—a system that projects a lattice of infrared dots into the environment and reads the distortions in that grid. When something—seen or unseen—interrupts the pattern, the software tries to map it as a human-like figure, often revealing forms standing where no person is visible.

Figure 28: Rem-Pod

They also deployed a Tesla coil, a compact instrument based on Nikola Tesla's early experiments with resonant electromagnetic fields. When activated, it fills the surrounding space with a pulsing, high-voltage charge of plasma in addition to a magnetic field. Some investigators believe this added energy can 'prime' a location, making anomalous activity easier to detect or even easier to manifest.

Another part of their toolkit was a Rem-Pod. This portable device emits a low-level radio-frequency field—a small bubble of energy—around its antenna. If anything enters or disturbs that field, visible or invisible, the device reacts instantly with alarm tones and flashing LEDs. Ninety-nine percent of the time when the Rem-Pod is deployed, nothing happens.

Ron also began experimenting with a green-light laser, a technology that produces a tightly focused beam of coherent light—light waves that all move in perfect alignment. Because of that precision, the green-light laser can project an exact grid or pinpoint onto a surface with almost no scatter. Ron used this property to energize specific areas with pinpoint accuracy.

Finally, they added their own thermal FLIR camera, a device that detects infrared radiation—the heat naturally emitted by objects, animals, and even cold voids, which have been known to indicate portals.

During their investigation, they used this suite of technologies to identify what they believed might be an interdimensional portal on the property. In their final experiment, the team attempted direct interaction with a nonhuman intelligence—an encounter captured not only on film but also through a computer-processed feed from a powerful magnetometer, which recorded simultaneous fluctuations in both electromagnetic and magnetic fields. Together, the visual and instrumental data suggested that something unseen was responding in real time.

Figure 29: FLIR Camera

* * *

Just as important as the new technologies was the fact that Ron and Alan began incorporating sensitives into their investigative team. For the Bradshaw Ranch expedition, Ron invited CJ Mulkerrin, a sensitive who had assisted the team in earlier investigations and had already visited the ranch on her own. She arrived with familiarity not only with the property but with its energetic landscape—the subtle pressures and impressions that investigators often overlook.

During the fourth day, the team chose to focus their investigation on what both local researchers and CJ described as a concentrated zone of high strangeness—a narrow space between the two ranch buildings. CJ guided them to a particular spot where, on previous visits, she had felt overwhelming nausea and a deep sense of unease. Standing there again, she felt it immediately. As did each of the team members. And it was in this exact location that the instruments registered something extraordinary: a possible interdimensional portal. The FLIR camera captured a sharply defined cold spot—an impossibility in the desert heat of midday—while the TriField EMF meter detected an intense magnetic bubble surrounding it. The overlap of sensory intuition and technological confirmation gave the moment an undeniable weight.

CJ was also present for the final experiment inside the ranch's main building when the team interacted with an alien entity. She added to the evidence of the interaction by recording the presence of a humanlike figure on her smart phone's camera using an SLS application.

Earlier that day, she had guided Alan to a quiet corner of the property where she sensed a Bigfoot presence. She explained that she often encountered them in dreams, and that one in particular had been trying to communicate. As Alan stood in the place she indicated, he felt an internal shift—an emotional pressure blooming in his chest, inexplicable yet unmistakable. CJ told him the message was simple: he had to open up even more.

* * *

The idea of working with psychics or sensitives was not new to the paranormal world, but within Bigfoot research it remained controversial. That began to change when pioneers like Thom Powell pushed the field forward. Powell—one of the earliest proponents of paranormal hotspots—had believed for a long time that Bigfoot was part of a larger paranormal ecology, and openly embraced the idea of engaging sensitives in his Bigfoot investigations. During the filming of an episode of the team's *Paranormal Highway* series on his property, he made his position unmistakably clear. To test this new direction, he invited one of his most trusted sensitives, Tish Paquette, to participate. Tish reported feeling the presence of Bigfoot on multiple occasions, sometimes even sensing entire families of them—beings she described as ancient guardians woven into the forest itself.

On the second night of filming, Tish led Alan down to a wooden bench where Powell himself had once encountered a presence he believed was Bigfoot. What happened next changed Alan's understanding of the phenomenon forever.

"I could feel the energy of this being walk up to me—probably within six feet. I was prepared for it to reach out and touch me. I could feel the energy; it was a warmth in my chest, and that warmth grew stronger until it began to swirl around me. I just felt the energy... and then it walked away. When we opened our eyes, the whole woods in front of us had a white glow to it."

That moment became a turning point in his evolution as both Bigfoot investigator and filmmaker. "The experience with Tish was mind-opening because, for the first time, I saw that I could interact with Sasquatch in a different way. What I learned is that it's very personal. The connection I had was for me—it was with me. It was a deeper level of feeling about this entity we'd been chasing for so long. And it made me realize there's something to this... some purpose to it. We're not just doing our thing and it's doing its thing—we're doing something together. That changed the game for me. And the purpose of it all."

After years of searching for the elusive Bigfoot, Alan was on the threshold of becoming a sensitive himself.

Looking back across this evolution—from wood knocks in the darkness to electromagnetic field readings at interdimensional portals —a pattern emerges. Each technological advancement, each new method of engagement, seemed to provoke a response from the phenomenon itself. The presence never simply submitted to documentation. Instead, it adapted, revealing itself in ways that matched the sophistication of the tools brought to bear.

Wood knocks answered wood knocks. Gifting sites produced impossibly placed gifts. FLIR cameras captured heat signatures that vanished before physical confirmation. Trail cams recorded creatures that flickered between dimensions. Magnetometers detected intelligent fluctuations that seemed aware of being measured.

The phenomenon stayed one step ahead, calibrating the mystery so investigators kept evolving toward it. It didn't hide from them—it engaged them through wonder, confusion, and the irresistible pull of the unknown. Its purpose, it seemed, wasn't to solve the mystery but to activate the minds that sought it.

The presence never answered the question. It reshaped the questioner.

5

ORACLES AND SENSITIVES

On the slopes of Mount Parnassus in Central Greece, overlooking the Pleistos Valley, lie the ruins of the most influential site in Western culture—the Oracle of Delphi. The sensitives were chosen from among local respectable women who vowed chastity and devoted their lives to the temple, serving as Apollo's mouthpiece for life. For a thousand years in ancient Greece, commoners and rulers alike visited the revered sanctuary, where a priestess of Apollo, known as the Pythia, delivered prophecies.

Figure 30: Oracle of Delphi Ruins; Photo by Tamara Semina at
Wikimedia Commons

To the ancient Greeks, Delphi was considered the center of the world, and as such was a doorway to the unknown, a portal by which the mysteries of life could be glimpsed. Often the Delphi Oracle's prophecies were ambiguous riddles or allegories, requiring interpretation by the seeker. This ambiguity was a key part of the oracle's mystique and power. But in another sense, the ambiguity itself laid a burden upon the listener and urged them to pierce the veil of mystery and seek clarity.

Figure 31: Oracle of Delphi; drawing by Heinrich Leutemann

Among the most famous of the Oracle's prophecies was the one given to King Croesus of Lydia, an empire located between present-day Greece and Turkey. Told that 'a great empire would fall' if he invaded Persia, he attacked, only to be defeated by Cyrus the Great, resulting in his own empire being destroyed.

The process for an Oracle to deliver her prophecies was simplicity itself. After purifying herself in sacred waters, a goat was sacrificed to the god Apollo. Then she was led into the temple, where she entered a trance induced by chewing laurel leaves. In some cases, it was believed that a chasm near the temple produced gases that had the same effect of inducing a trance in the priestess.

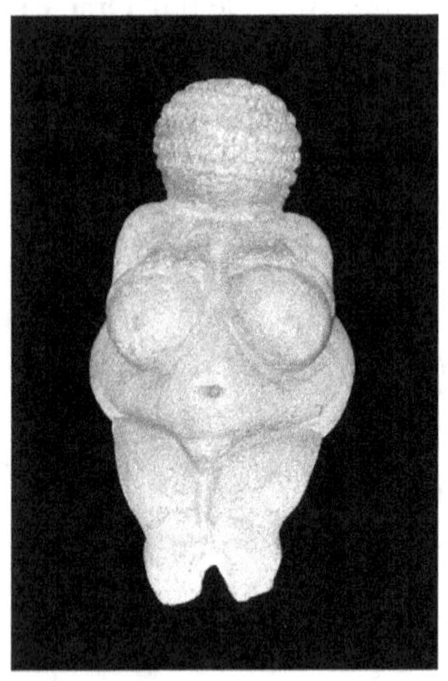

Figure 32: Venus of Dolni Vestonice – Photo by Petr Novák Wikipedia

However the transition was accomplished, the Oracle entered the trance-like state which enabled her to keep one foot secure in this world while visiting the next.

The Oracle of Delphi is just one example of the role of sensitives throughout humankind's existence on Earth. However, the history of sensitives predates the Greeks by tens of thousands of years.

The extensive discovery of Venus Figurines across Eurasia, dating from 40,000 to 10,000 years ago, would seem to indicate that early modern humans of the Upper Paleolithic sought guidance from revered women regarding fertility and childbearing. A popular theory among archaeologists is that these statuettes are effigies of a Great Mother Goddess or Earth Mother deity, venerated as the source of all life, growth, and the cycle of death and rebirth in nature. This potential deity may represent one of the most ancient and longest-worshipped figures in human history.

In modern antiquity, Western civilization has had a great many oracles in addition to the Oracle of Delphi,

Figure 33:Nostradamus by his son Cesar

including the Oracle of Dodona, dedicated to Zeus; the Oracle of Amun in the Siwa Oasis, which Alexander the Great visited; and the Sibylline Oracles, a collection of prophecies consulted by the Romans.

Figure 34: Edgar Cayce, Wikimedia Commons

Post-Biblical oracles include such luminaries as Michel de Nostredame, known by his Latinized name Nostradamus. He was a French astrologer, apothecary, physician, and reputed seer best known for his book *Les Prophéties*, a collection of 942 poetic quatrains predicting future events. Like the Oracle of Delphi, Nostradamus's quatrains are ambiguous, leading scholars to enter the realm of mystery in order to find some interpretation for their meaning.

In the 20th century, seers Edgar Cayce and Jeane Dixon were renowned for their predictions, including the stock market crash of 1929, World War II, and the assassination of JFK.

And in the 21st century, the Nechung Oracle is the official state oracle for the government of Tibet and is still regularly consulted by the Dalai Lama. The Dalai Lama also consults the Tenma Oracle, for which a young Tibetan woman named Khandro La serves as the medium for several mountain goddesses.

Figure 35: Jeanne Dixon, Wikimedia Commons

Finally, the word 'oracle' in contemporary terms is often used metaphorically to describe sources of information that provide insight into the future, although without a supernatural connotation. For example, recent Artificial Intelligence (AI) systems like ChatGPT have been described as modern oracles because they can provide information and potential scenarios based on vast amounts of data, tapping into the human desire for quick answers and the ability to predict the future.

However, the acceptance of sensitives with a unique talent to see beneath the reality of our five senses, to pierce the veil into the next world, was—until the second half of the 20th century—negligible. Indeed, many people called them frauds, among them Harry Houdini. The famous magician and escape artist spent much of his later life exposing charlatans who used séances to supposedly speak with the dead.

Figure 36: Harry Houdini, Wikimedia Commons

This historical bridge from specially anointed individuals interpreting the will of the gods to the subtleties of 21st-century people begins in the 1970s with the emergence of the New Age Movement, or the age of Aquarius.

Interestingly, as Ron and Alan's team discovered later, Saint-Germain, a sensitive and Oracle from the 18th-century European aristocracy is credited with predicting the arrival of the Age of Aquarius—a global era of freedom and unity—and is said to have gifted humanity the Violet Flame (a spiritual energy of purification) to help achieve this new age.[1]

The New Age Movement provided unyielding support in some communities for Highly Sensitive People (HSPs), such as Tish Paquette and CJ Mulkerrin—individuals with a heightened response to sensory input and emotional stimuli. At the same time, the rise of subtle energy sensitives in the New Age movement perfectly demonstrates Jacques Vallée's Control System hypothesis adapting to the needs and vocabulary of modern, for a possible post-religious society.

---

1. The enigmatic 18th century European adventurer, alchemist, and musician, the Comte de Saint-Germain, is believed by some to be immortal or an Ascended Master, connected to secret societies and spiritual teachings.

In Vallée's hypothesis, sensitives function as interpreters—human interfaces between ordinary reality and the Control System itself. They serve as conduits through which information flows, translating inexplicable phenomena into culturally acceptable narratives. HSPs are the latest iteration of this Controlled Information Channel, managing the mystery through subjective, difficult-to-verify experiential knowledge. The Control System requires these interpreters because direct, unambiguous contact would collapse the mystery entirely— and the mystery itself appears to be the mechanism of control.

Figure 37: Engraving of the Comte de Saint-Germain by Nicholas Thomas in the Louvre

The Esalen Institute,[2] founded by Michael Murphy and Richard Price, was ground zero for America's New Age Movement and was frequented by many well-known leaders of the Human Potential Movement, including Ansel Adams, Buckminster Fuller, Timothy Leary, Linus Pauling, Carl Rogers, Abraham Maslow, Fritz Perls, Alan Watts, Joseph Campbell, Ram Dass, Terence McKenna, Ida Rolf, Moshe Feldenkrais, Hunter S. Thompson, Joan Baez, Aldous Huxley and George Leonard.[3] Rather than merely lecturing, many leaders experi-

---

2. For more information on the Esalen Institute read *Esalen: America and the Religion of No Religion* written by Jeffrey J. Kripal, a scholar of comparative religion who details the institute's history, its role in the human potential movement, and its unique blend of Eastern spirituality and Western science. Kripal, a former board chair of Esalen, explores the founders' vision and the institute's impact on culture, psychology, and spirituality.

3. George Leonard, who was a close friend of Ron Meyer, is often referred to as the 'Third Founder' of the Esalen Institute. Leonard was the primary intellectual architect who helped frame its mission and introduced it to the mainstream American public. As a senior editor for *Look* magazine, Leonard wrote a seminal piece titled 'The Human Potential,' which gave the entire movement its name. His journalistic reach brought Esalen's ideas to a readership of millions. He also served as both Vice President and President of the Esalen Institute, providing leadership during its most formative decades.

mented with what Huxley called the non-verbal humanities: the education of the body, the senses, and the emotions. Their intention was to help individuals develop awareness of their present flow of experience, to express this fully and accurately, and to listen to feedback.

During and after the cultural shifts of the 1960s and 70s, the concepts of subtle bodies and energies became the dominant language for sensitives, shifting the focus from external deities (such as in the Oracle of Delphi) to unrealized potential of humans through the insights and practices of the Human Potential Movement.

The modern sensitive carries the torch of history by interpreting Non-Human Intelligence's presence through an energetic, rather than a scientific or religious, lens. And those who demonstrate true abilities have had a profound impact on modern society.

Modern-day sensitives arrive at their capabilities through various paths. Some are born with heightened perception, aware from childhood that they experience the world differently from others. For others, the abilities emerge over time, gradually sharpening through practice and attention. Still others awaken to these gifts only after a significant transformative experience—a near-death experience, a spiritual awakening, or even a direct contact with Bigfoot or other Non-Human Intelligence. The trauma or transcendence of such encounters can tear open perceptual doors that were previously closed, permanently altering how an individual processes reality.

The age of the sensitive has involved several iterations, including crystal gazers, mediums, shamans, chakra readers, and healers. Some of these New Age sensitives exert a kind of psychological control, interpreting a person's 'dark' or 'light' energy fields and directing personal growth and anxiety by externalizing internal issues as 'bad energy,' reinforcing the need for continuous external or internal correction. Others are channelers or mediums who receive messages from Ascended Masters or Extraterrestrial Guides.Still more HSPs are ley line dowsers and vortex seekers who can feel powerful or negative energies at sacred sites such as Mount Shasta.[4]

---

4. Ley line dowsers use dowsing techniques, such as rods and pendulums, to find invisi-

Figure 38: Ley Lines at Malvern Hills United Kingdom described by Alfred Watkins, amateur English archaeologist who developed the idea of ley lines.

And then there are folk seers who identify and sanctify specific geographical nodes as places where the veil between this world and the next is thin, associating strange happenings such as UAPs and Bigfoot with a natural, ancient, energetic principle, thereby normalizing the anomaly within a paranormal context.

What makes the modern sensitive particularly compelling, and particularly relevant to the Bigfoot phenomenon, is that their experiences don't end with passive perception. Sensitives frequently report that energetic phenomena lead to action, to interaction, and even to communication. The presence they sense often guides them, directs them, or delivers specific messages meant for others. A good example of this is when sensitive CJ Mulkerrin interpreted a message from the Bigfoot presence at Bradshaw Ranch for Alan Megargle to open up more.

This kind of interaction reveals something crucial about the role of sensitives. They are not merely detectors or observers. They are partic-

---

ble, energetic pathways called ley lines, believed to connect sacred sites or carry Earth's natural power. Vortex seekers are people drawn to Earth's powerful swirling energies, known as energy vortexes, in places like Sedona, Arizona.

ipants in a dynamic exchange with the phenomenon. The energetic presence doesn't just *appear*—it *engages*. It gives direction. It assigns tasks. It uses the sensitive as a bridge to influence others who may not possess the same heightened perception. Indeed, in addition to the sensitives at Bradshaw Ranch, Alan and Ron's team used sensitives at Oklahoma, Church Creek and Mt. Shasta to open the group to the subtle energies present and to heighten the group's experience.

Figure 39a: Juergen Hess using dowsing rods at Bradshaw Ranch to demonstrate the effect of a portal

This active, reciprocal relationship between sensitive and the Bigfoot phenomenon is exactly what Vallée's Control System hypothesis of an ancient presence always keeping the mystery alive would predict. If the goal of the Control System is to subtly influence human belief, behavior, and culture, then sensitives are translators—mediums through which cryptic signals become actionable insight. The phenomenon reveals itself just enough to be noticed, but never so clearly that it can be pinned down. The sensitive interprets, relays, and validates the experience, ensuring the mystery remains alive while nudging individuals and groups in specific directions.

All of these New Age Sensitives contribute to the great mystery of humanity through a kind of mythological steerage. Their experiences and interpretations flood the public sphere with complex, non-verifiable cosmic lore, constantly updating the narrative to keep the human imagination engaged—to keep humans chasing after the mystery, looking for answers.

The claim that sensitives can feel the presence of Bigfoot and its families fits the hypothesis perfectly. It transforms the elusive physical cryptid into an energetic being or 'guardian of the forest.' This dual nature—physical yet spiritual—makes definitive proof impossible and reinforces the necessity of the sensitive's subjective experience to access the truth.

One drawback from society's hyper-awareness of sensitives, however, is the Industry of Ambiguity. The capacity of so many individuals to 'sense energies' has spawned a global industry—crystals, aura readings, vortex tours, healing systems. This commodification ensures the phenomenon remains subjective and non-scientific. If the experience were easily quantifiable, it would lose its economic and spiritual mystique.

In addition, the New Age movement spawned scores of charlatans —self-proclaimed psychics with no real power; gurus who built cults using psychological manipulation and financial exploitation; fraudulent 'healers' promoting dangerous, unproven cures; and unscrupulous marketers selling everything from toxic snake oil remedies to exorbitantly priced, useless 'spiritual' merchandise. These predators make it even harder to validate or prove real sensitives' abilities.

Nevertheless, the modern sensitive is thus a crucial component of keeping the mystery alive. They are the individuals who translate the chaotic, anomalous signals into a socially palatable, psychologically absorbing, and commercially viable narrative, while at the same time refuting the bulwark of the scientific community's attempts to criticize it. More than passive receivers, they are active participants—guided, directed, and sometimes commanded by the very phenomena they claim to interpret.

6

CHURCH CREEK

It had been more than two years since the object came crashing through the trees in Oklahoma, and Ron Meyer had quietly decided his search for understanding the nature of Bigfoot was over. The event had been too bizarre, too impossible, too far outside any framework he could reasonably defend. Whatever Bigfoot was, it was no longer plausible to think of it as a biological animal—a hidden human, a relict hominid, or an undiscovered great ape avoiding exposure. That explanation no longer fit the evidence.

And yet, the phenomenon itself refused to loosen its grip. Bigfoot remained compelling not because it could be proven, but because it could not be dismissed. Its pull was not scientific so much as existential—an unanswered question pressing at the edges of meaning.

Then, in the summer of 2025, Alan Megargle and his team, including his wife Anna Megargle took two paranormal authors on what was supposed to be an ordinary Bigfoot search to a quiet, unremarkable stretch of wilderness known as the Church Creek site.

The Church Creek site lies near the small mountain town of Bailey, Colorado—long considered the center of reported Bigfoot activity in the Rocky Mountains. Despite that reputation, the Church Creek site itself was largely a classic piece of Rocky Mountains wilderness hidden deep within the Pike-San Isabel National Forests. The area sits far from regular traffic, development, or infrastructure. There are no nearby homes, no cell towers, no persistent sounds of human activity. Once inside the trees, the modern world falls away quickly.

The landscape is dominated by distinctive massive Pikes Peak granite formations,[1] with aspen groves and dry stands of ponderosa pine climbing the high-altitude slopes. Clear freshwater creeks cut through the terrain, shaping narrow corridors of green in an otherwise rugged environment. Elk, mule deer, black bears, and mountain lions move through the area as they have for centuries. Human presence here is minimal and temporary; the ecosystem belongs overwhelmingly to the wildlife that inhabits it.

Figure 40: Aerial view of Church Creek and the Pikes Peak granite formations

At the heart of this region sits the Sasquatch Outpost in Bailey, owned and operated by Jim Myers. For years, Myers has guided people on Bigfoot expeditions on foot and horseback, occasionally leading small groups into the Church Creek area as part of those outings. A short distance from the outpost lies the historic Glen Isle Resort, a property listed on the National Register of Historic Places. Since 2019, it has served as the base for the annual Bigfoot Adventure Weekend, organized each summer by Alan Megargle, Jesse Morgan, and Jim

---

1. Pikes Peak's formations are primarily the ancient, billion-year-old Pikes Peak granite, a pinkish igneous rock that cooled underground and was later pushed up and exposed, then sculpted by uplift, glaciers, and erosion into distinctive rounded domes and jagged peaks.

Myers. As part of those events, participants have also been taken into Church Creek on occasion—brief visits, limited in scope, after which the forest quickly reclaimed its silence.

Despite these repeated entries into the area, nothing unusual had ever occurred there—at least nothing that could be clearly connected to Bigfoot.

Figure 41: Church Creek site Map 1

The physical layout of the site reinforces its isolation. A single parking area marks the last obvious sign of human access. From there, a trail heads west, gradually disappearing as it follows Church Creek deeper into the forest. In another direction, the land opens briefly into a wide meadow before sloping down toward the creek, its banks lined with small trees and dense shrubs. Beyond that, there are no paths, no signs, and no reason for anyone to be there unless they are looking for something.

* * *

It was at this site, on a crisp summer evening, that Alan and his team were asked to lead what was intended to be a routine investigation for two well-known writers: Erin Taylor and Richard Estep.

Taylor, a Colorado-based author and paranormal investigator with nearly two decades of experience, had come looking for something beyond the page. Known within the paranormal community for her books and fieldwork exploring unexplained phenomena, she had spent years documenting strange encounters—but like many investigators, she remained open to the possibility that certain locations might still hold something more.

Figure 42:Richard Estep performing a wood knock

Richard Estep brought a similarly seasoned perspective, though from a slightly different angle. With more than thirty years of research into hauntings and unexplained occurrences on both sides of the Atlantic, Estep had authored numerous books examining the intersection of history, folklore and the paranormal. His voice was familiar to audiences interested in the deeper cultural implications of mystery.

Both were drawn to the area by its reputation as a center of Sasquatch activity. Team member Jesse Morgan had described the area as a kind of Bigfoot heart—a place where reports clustered and strange events seemed to concentrate.

The group meandered along the Church Creek trail, listening carefully, scanning the tree line, watching for any hint of movement.

Nothing happened.

They paused. Richard attempted a traditional wood knock, striking a tree with deliberate force, hoping for a response.

There was none.

Jesse tried another familiar tactic—one often reported in Sasquatch encounters—a long, deliberate howl meant not to provoke, but to invite acknowledgment.

Still nothing.

As full darkness settled in, Alan decided to try something different. He placed a REM-Pod on the ground—an unconventional tool for Bigfoot research, but one the team had been experimenting with for over a year. The device emits a small electromagnetic field and activates when something enters it, a technology more commonly associated with ghost investigations.

After positioning the REM-Pod, the group stood quietly while Alan led a brief mindfulness meditation, emphasizing calm intention rather than expectation.

Then the REM-Pod triggered.

Anna spoke first, addressing the unseen presence directly. "Would you please step away?"

The REM-Pod shut off.

To test the interaction, Alan calmly asked whatever was there to step back into the field.

The REM-Pod activated again.

Anna stared at the device. "It's starting again."

Alan asked, "Still going?"

"Yeah," she said. "Constantly. That's unusual."

Alan suggested she request distance once more, and Anna asked, "Could you step away for a second?" Moments later she reported, "It stopped."

However, the silence was short-lived. Within a minute, the REM-Pod activated again with its characteristic pattern of beeps, tones and flashing lights.

Richard stepped forward, clearly intent on engaging whatever was interacting with the device. "Would you move away from the REM-Pod and come toward me, please?"

After a few seconds, the device went silent.

"Thank you," Richard said. In his unmistakable British drawl, he continued, "Would you be kind enough to step back into the REM-Pod field?"

Figure 43: Richard Estep interacting with an entity through the REM-POD

Almost immediately, the device activated again. At the same time, the microphone picked up what sounded like footsteps moving across the ground.

"Thank you very much," Richard said, visibly astonished.

After about thirty seconds, the REM-Pod shut off again. Wanting to test the limits of the interaction with this invisible entity, Richard made one final request. "Would you please stay back for fifty heartbeats, and then enter the field?"

He counted aloud on camera. When he reached fifty, the REM-Pod activated once more.

Richard froze. "Oh my God. Are you shitting me?" he said, his British aplomb evaporating.

Back at the parking lot, Richard and Erin reflected on what had just occurred. "I don't even know how to explain that," she admitted. "Something was interacting with us—but who or what that was is still unknown."

"We certainly interacted with something," Richard said. "As both Anna and Erin have said, what it was is open to debate. But it responded when we invited it in. I'm really glad I came out tonight."

That night, however, was only the beginning of what Church Creek had in store.

* * *

The next event would involve Kenny Collins, known across Colorado as Mr. Bigfoot. Kenny had spent decades searching for Sasquatch, carrying with him an almost childlike hope

that the mystery might one day meet him halfway. When he heard about the Church Creek experience, he asked Alan to meet him at the site. Alan agreed, bringing Anna along.

Kenny was already familiar with the area, having led groups through the trails during previous Bigfoot weekends. He arrived early that afternoon and ventured into the Church Creek wilderness alone.

Figure 44: Kenny Collins

When Alan and Anna reached the site, Alan began walking along the tree line holding a camera, searching for Kenny. Suddenly, Alan felt it—a presence. He heard something and whistled.

Almost immediately, there was a reply. Two sharp wood knocks echoed back—distinct, deliberate and close. Not footsteps. Not branch snaps. Something intentional. Later, back in the studio, audio analysis would confirm the impression. The sound did not resemble animal movement or environmental noise. Its audio impulses were consistent with wood striking wood.

Anna caught up with Alan and began filming as he met up with Kenny.

"So what did you hear?" Alan asked.

"I heard something like ou-gou-o," Kenny said. "It lasted long enough to make me turn. You were looking the same way. We both heard it. It was awesome."

"But there's nobody out here," Alan said, bewildered by the sound.

"Right," Kenny replied.

Because Anna had been some distance away, her microphone captured only part of the sound. Still, audio analysis suggested something unusual—vowel-like tones, human-style in structure, but inconsistent with known animal calls or radio-frequency artifacts.

Figure 45: Kenny Collins tells Alan Megargle he heard AEIOU

Alan turned to the camera and explained what happened. "Kenny was up on the hillside over there. We were walking back down, just talking, when something behind us started making sounds—woo, woh, woo—like the so-called Samurai-style Bigfoot chatter.[2] Kenny and I both froze. Whatever it was stopped us instantly."

Back at the parking lot, Alan and Kenny reflected on what they had heard.

"What did it sound like to you?" Alan asked.

"It sounded like more than one vowel," Kenny said. "It sounded like A E I O U."

Alan stared at him in amazement. "That's what you heard?"

"Now that I can process it," Kenny said, "yeah, that's what it was."

A look of realization crossed Alan's face. "So you don't know about that," he said quietly to Anna. "I didn't even think of it—but he's right. When Ron and I were in Oklahoma two years ago, he taught me a chant. We did it five times, and a rock was thrown at us. The chant was AEIOU."

The implications were staggering. These vowels had been repeated hundreds of miles apart. And what did it mean that a sound resembling proto-language—an ancient vowel structure echoed in human chanting—had emerged here at Church Creek, wrapped in the same tonal quality as the legendary Sierra Sounds? Even more unsettling was the implication that whatever produced the sound seemed to know it would be understood.

The vocalization was not random. It was not merely noise.

---

2. The audio recordings known as the Sierra Sounds—sometimes called the Samurai Sounds, a colloquial term coined because the vocalizations reminded some listeners of the intense, pseudo-archaic Japanese dialogue heard in old samurai films—remain among the most controversial and compelling pieces of acoustic evidence in Bigfoot research. Captured beginning in 1971 by Ron Morehead and Alan Berry in California's Sierra Nevada mountains, the recordings include rapid, complex vocalizations unlike known human or animal sounds. Linguistic analysis suggests the vocal tract required to produce them would need to be longer than that of a modern human. These recordings challenge the idea of Bigfoot as a solitary brute and instead suggest social complexity and proto-linguistic capability. To this day, the Sierra Sounds remain the gold standard in Sasquatch acoustic evidence.

It was as if the presence—whether Bigfoot or some Non-Human Intelligence—had reached into a shared symbolic vocabulary, selecting a pattern Alan and Kenny would recognize.

The mystery took on a new dimension. Not just a phenomenon making itself known—but one demonstrating awareness.

* * *

One week after first hearing the AEIOU chant, Alan, Anna, and Jesse returned to Church Creek, hoping to capture a clear audio recording. What they encountered instead was something even more unsettling. The telling of their experience reads like an episode of the television series *The Mystery of Skinwalker Ranch.*

The team walked slowly along the creek, stopping periodically to listen but hearing nothing. Eventually, the group split up. Alan crossed to the south side of the creek, while Jesse and Anna—camera in hand —continued along the north side.

Then, without warning, both noticed a strange odor.

"I smell it," Jesse said. "Is there a campfire? Maybe far away?"

"It smells like crap," Anna replied.

Numerous Bigfoot witnesses have reported encounters accompanied by powerful, unusual odors—rotting flesh, sulfur, skunk-like musk.

They continued sniffing the air. Then the odor changed.

"It's almost sweet at the same time," Jesse observed.

Bigfoot reports also include rare moments when the air turns oddly fragrant—honeysuckle, lilac, something floral and completely out of place.

As quickly as the smell appeared, it vanished.

"I can't even describe what that was," Jesse said.

"It's bizarre," Anna added.

The abrupt disappearance only deepened the sense that something unseen was moving through the space—close enough to be sensed, yet impossible to locate. Then they heard the clear, distinct, unmistakable sounds of Bigfoot chatter.

Figure 46: Jesse Morgan asking Alan Megargle if he heard the Samurai chatter

Shaken, Jesse grabbed his walkie-talkie and called Alan. "Did you hear that weird fucking noise?"

"No," Alan replied. "What did it sound like?"

"That gibberish talk—the Samurai Bigfoot chatter."

Later audio analysis broke the sound into components: A breathy murmur—*uhhh*—rising into a bright *ee*—then falling rough, like *roh*. To the human ear, it formed a single fluid expression: *Uh-yee-rohh.*

Another vowel-rich vocalization. Not a present-day, known language, but proto-speech. Sounds that were language-like. More importantly, the team had experienced another reminder that whatever was happening at Church Creek was no longer content to remain silent.

* * *

The following week, Anna told her father, Ron, about the connection. She explained how the AEIOU chant he had used in Oklahoma— almost casually, two years earlier—had surfaced again at Church Creek. How Kenny and Alan had independently heard the same sequence of vowels, spoken not by a human voice, but by something moving just beyond the tree line.

Anna took out her phone. "I want to show you something," she explained. "This is what Jesse and I recorded at Church Creek. You'll hear a bark first. Then something else."

Ron listened. "Can I hear that again? That's crazy."

She played it a second time. "There's like a growl and then what we think might be Bigfoot."

Ron smiled in recognition. "It sounds like the Sierra Sounds. The recordings Ron Morehead captured."

Anna smiled also and said, "So, we were thinking of taking you out there."

For the first time in more than two years, Ron felt something stir that he had not felt since his last field investigation—the pull of a synchronicity. "I'm actually looking forward to it," he said. "That'd be cool."

Later, in the audio lab, the recording was analyzed. The structure stood out immediately: not animal, not random, not environmental. Indeed, the vocalization showed internal structure. It was then that something clicked.

For months, Ron had been researching frontier Large Language Models (LLMs) for a novel he was writing—artificial intelligence systems built entirely on statistical relationships between symbols. Their amazing output did not come from understanding, only from predictions. Pattern completion.

Some AI researchers suggested the radical idea that human language itself may work the same way. Structure came first and meaning followed. Pattern before thinking and talking.

Listening again to the Church Creek audio, Ron felt the floor shift beneath him. What if the Bigfoot phenomenon was pointing to language and its origin—the beginning of everything we call human? It was as if something in the guise of Bigfoot at Church Creek was saying: *Look here. Look at language.*

* * *

Figure 47: Ron Meyer and Alan Megargle performing AEIOU chant

The following weekend, Alan and Anna took Ron to Church Creek. The plan was simple: attempt to record additional vocalizations or any other unusual interactions tied to the anomalous presence at the site. For Ron, it was also a chance to try the AEIOU chant again—this time in the place where the vowels had answered back.

Together, the three performed the chant seven times, however, with no mindfulness meditation. As before, Alan crossed to the south side of the creek while Anna, followed by Ron, remained on the north side. At one point, Ron stopped to rest as Anna continued ahead alone. It was Anna who heard it and recorded it. Again, nobody else was around.

Audio analysis later revealed a short, male baritone utterance—two syllables, perfectly repeated twice: *Hoh-rah... Hoh-rah.*

The repetition was exact. As before, the sounds were not noise, nor artifact, nor animal. Moreover, the sounds implied intention.

When Alan and Anna eventually returned to the parking lot, Ron was waiting. For reasons he could not articulate, Alan decided to test his new night-vision camera. A night-vision camera works by shining and amplifying invisible near-infrared light reflected by physical surfaces, unlike thermal imaging, which detects heat.

Figure 48: Alan Megargle looking through his night vision camera

Alan scanned the tree line along Church Creek where the earlier encounters had occurred. Then he stopped. "There's something in there," he whispered. "I can see one of the eyes reflecting back at me."

The camera clearly captured what Alan was seeing: a single point of infrared light, stationary and fixed.

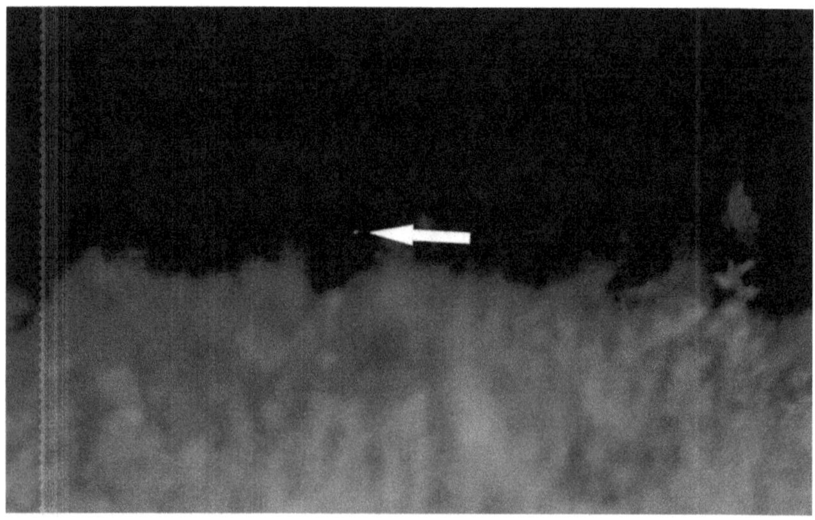

Figure 49: Light source through the night vision camera along the Church Creek treeline

Alan handed the camera to Anna, and she guided him toward the source. As Alan approached, the light remained visible on the screen. But when he reached the exact location, nothing was there. No reflective surface, no animal, and more mysteriously, no explanation. Yet the light persisted in the camera's view, seen by Anna and Ron, hovering precisely where something should have been. The anomaly remained visible, unmoving, as if the camera itself were being allowed to see something the human eye could not.

Then it vanished.

Two weeks later, Ron had an epiphany.

7

THE ORIGIN OF
NATURAL LANGUAGE

Long before humans spoke, the world was already alive with communication.

Biologists now recognize that nearly all living systems exchange information. Birds sing complex songs to mark territory and attract mates. Whales communicate across hundreds of miles of ocean using patterned, low-frequency calls. Wolves coordinate hunts through posture, scent, and sound. Even insects participate in symbolic exchange: bees perform precise dances encoding the location of food, while ants leave chemical trails that function as collective memory. Octopuses flash color patterns across their skin.

At still deeper levels of life, communication persists. Once a population reaches a critical threshold, bacteria exchange chemical signals in quorum sensing, altering collective behavior.[1] Slime molds—organisms without brains—can solve mazes and optimize paths through distributed signaling alone.

And yet, despite this astonishing spectrum of biological communication, only one species on Earth developed a spoken natural language —humans.

Natural language—the kind humans use—isn't just about making sounds. Animals make sounds all the time. What makes human language unique is that it's a structured system built from small,

---

1. Quorum sensing is a bacterial cell-to-cell communication system that allows microbes to sense their population density by releasing and detecting chemical signals called autoinducers; when these signals reach a critical concentration—a 'quorum'— bacteria collectively change gene expression to coordinate group behaviors like forming biofilms, or producing toxins.

discrete building blocks that we call words. These words don't just exist in isolation. They unfold in a specific sequence, one after another, and each word depends on what came before it. There's an internal architecture—invisible rules—that determines what can meaningfully come next. Linguists have a technical term for this: syntax.

But there's another way of thinking about it that's become popular in recent years, especially with the rise of artificial intelligence. Cognitive scientists now describe language as having an 'autoregressive structure.' That's a fancy way of saying that meaning emerges step by step, moment by moment, as each element conditions what comes next. It's like a chain reaction of meaning, with each link determining the shape of the one that follows.

For this kind of system to arise among early humans, two critical conditions had to be met. First, there had to be a community—a group of people large enough and stable enough to share and preserve this linguistic architecture over time. You can't have language with just one person. It's inherently social. Language requires mutual participation, constant reinforcement, and gentle correction when someone gets it wrong. A single speaker, alone on an island, cannot create or sustain language. But a culture? A culture absolutely can.

The second condition was purely physical. The human body—specifically the human nervous system—had to evolve the biological machinery capable of producing and perceiving a very specific range of sounds. This meant developing extraordinarily fine motor control over the muscles of the mouth, throat, and tongue. It also meant evolving ears sensitive enough to detect subtle variations in pitch, duration, and resonance—differences that can completely change the meaning of a word.

Over countless generations, as human communities grew and their physiology adapted, something remarkable emerged from this convergence: a small set of foundational sounds that would become the backbone of all human speech. We call them vowels.

Across all known spoken languages, vowel sounds form the acoustic backbone of speech. They are open, resonant tones produced without obstructing airflow. Linguists often represent them with the familiar symbols A, E, I, O, and U—not because these letters are universal, but because the sounds themselves are. These are the sounds that carry speech forward. They bind consonants together. They sustain rhythm. Without them, language collapses into a guttural noise. It was these very sounds—stripped of words, grammar, or cultural markers— that were heard and recorded at the Church Creek site.

During multiple nighttime investigations, microphones captured a sequence of repeated, vowel-like vocalizations: long, breath-supported tones cycling through sounds closely resembling A ... E ... I ... O ... U. Interwoven with these were bursts of rapid, modulated chatter that was rhythmic, patterned, and non-random.

The recordings bore a striking similarity to what are known as the Sierra Sounds[2], captured decades earlier in the mountains of California. Those sounds—still unmatched and unexplained—are widely regarded as the only known example of a natural language-like vocalization that does not belong to any human linguistic family on Earth. They are not animal calls. They do not conform to primate vocal ranges. And they do not map onto any known human language— ancient or modern. Yet they exhibit structure.

The Church Creek recordings added something new. The presence of sustained vowel sequences—unadorned, almost instructional in their repetition—suggested not conversation, but the demonstration of a nonhuman presence. Not communication within a language, but attention drawn to the preconditions of language itself.

For most of human history, language existed only as fleeting sounds. Archaeological evidence suggests that anatomically modern humans developed the physical capacity for spoken language between 100,000 and 200,000 years ago, as changes in the hyoid bone, vocal

---

2. Recorded by Ron Morehead and Al Berry starting in 1971 during remote wilderness expeditions, the Sierra Sounds are audio recordings capturing Bigfoot vocalizations in the Sierra Nevada mountains, featuring distinct, multi-toned sounds, including distinctive whoops, growls, and complex, language-like phrases—often referred to as 'Samurai Chatter'—by multiple entities, and what some experts call non-human, complex communication. Spectral analysis reportedly shows frequencies and vocal ranges beyond normal human capabilities. They are considered the audio equivalent of the famous Patterson-Gimlin film and remain a significant, debated topic in cryptozoology.

tract, and auditory cortex made sustained, nuanced speech possible. But physical capacity alone was not enough. Language required time—many thousands of years of shared use—to stabilize into recognizable patterns.

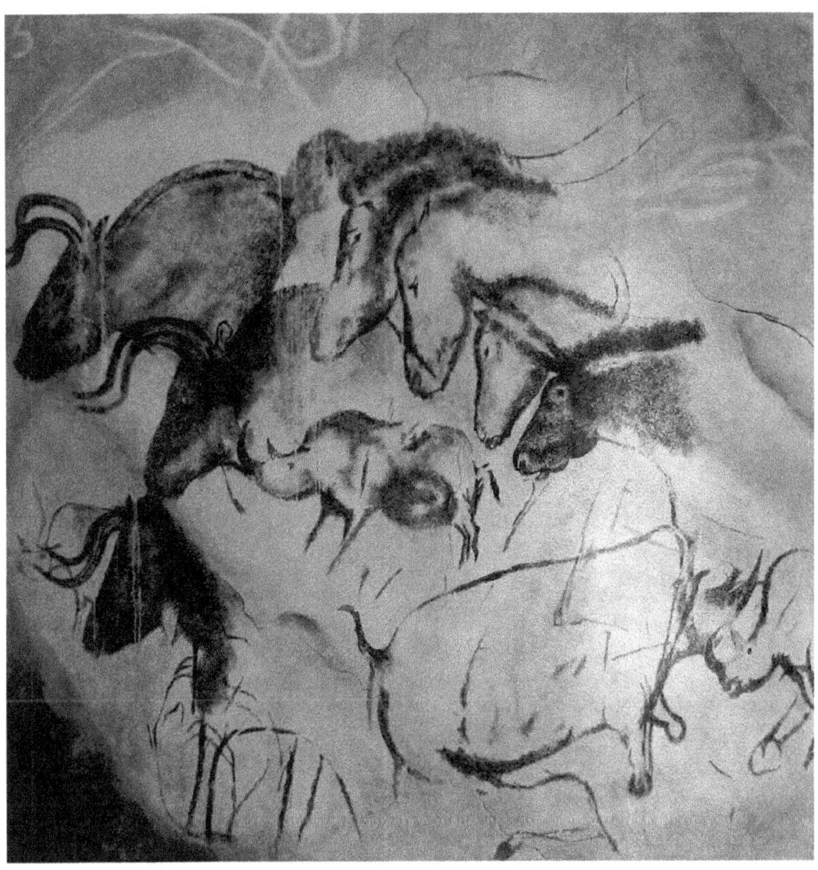

Figure 50: Painting from the Chauvet-Pont-d'Arc cave in Southeastern France

The earliest spoken languages have left no direct trace. Sound does not fossilize. What remains instead are indirect markers: increasingly complex tools, coordinated hunting strategies, symbolic objects, and ritual behavior. By 70,000 years ago, cave art and personal ornaments appear across Africa and Eurasia, strongly suggesting that language had become sophisticated enough to transmit myth, memory, and meaning across generations.

Speech transformed human time. Experience could be narrated. The past could be preserved. The future could be imagined. Knowledge no longer died with the individual—it moved, invisibly, from mind to mind.

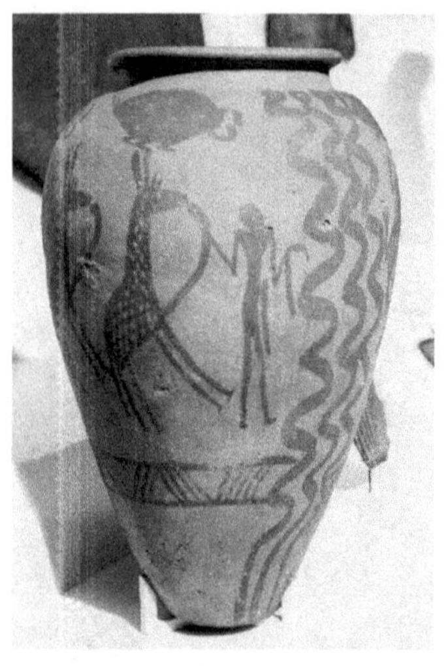

Figure 51: Paintings with symbols on Naqada II pottery circa 3500-3200 BCE by Einsamer Schütze at the Ägyptisches Museum, Berlin - Wikimedia Commons

Yet spoken language remained fragile. It existed only in the moment of utterance. Words vanished as soon as they were spoken, surviving only through repetition and collective memory. Cultures developed elaborate techniques to compensate for language's inherent fragility: epic poetry, song, chant, and rhythm. Long before writing, memory was trained through sound.

This is why early language and music are inseparable. Chant stabilized speech. Rhythm made language durable. Repetition turned fleeting sounds into something that could endure.

It is no coincidence that many of the oldest surviving linguistic structures—prayers, invocations, and origin stories—are rhythmic, vowel-rich, and often sung rather than spoken. Sound itself became a storage medium.

But eventually, sound was not enough. As human societies grew larger and more complex, spoken language reached its limits. Trade networks expanded. Agricultural calendars demanded precision. Laws and lineages required permanence. Around 5,000 years ago, in multiple regions of the world, language made a decisive shift–it became visible.

The earliest writing systems emerged independently, as early as 3300 BCE, in Sumer, Egypt, the Indus Valley, and 2000 years later in China and Mesoamerica. These first marks were not literature. They were records. In the case of the Egyptians, the earliest hieroglyphs appeared on bone or ivory tags and pottery. They were used initially for labeling goods and recording administrative details, evolving from proto-literate symbols into a full writing system as society grew complex. Writing did not begin as expression—it began as control.

What is striking is that writing did not replace speech. It abstracted it. Symbols stood in for sounds. Sounds stood in for meaning. Meaning stood in for reality. Each step increased distance from the source, but also power. Information could now outlive the speaker. Authority could persist beyond the human voice.

52: Hieroglyphs from the Tomb of Seti I by Jon Bodsworth at the British Museum

Over time, writing systems evolved from pictographs to phonetic scripts. Symbols no longer represented things—they represented sounds. In effect, writing learned to speak. By the time alphabetic systems appeared, language had been fully externalized. Thought could now move without a body. Memory no longer required a brain. Indeed, language had escaped the human skull.

The consequences were profound. Writing enabled bureaucracy, religion, mathematics, and eventually science to flourish. It allowed cultures to grow beyond what any group of individuals could remember. But it also introduced a new asymmetry: those who controlled written language controlled history ... controlled reality.

For millennia, this architecture remained stable and humans became amazing storytellers, relating stories about what humans are ... their place in the universe ... and what is truth and reality.

* * *

Spanning survival, entertainment, and identity, storytelling is a uniquely sophisticated human activity. While its forms evolve, its essence remains constant: not just to inform, but to connect and provide a framework for understanding the world.

To understand how storytelling evolved, let's step back in time, to the moment when humanity's oral tradition began ... to the moment when humans took the thoughts swirling about in their minds and recorded them for others to see.

The history of storytelling is as old as humanity, beginning with cave paintings—like Chauvet in modern-day southern France (circa) 40,000 BCE—to teach survival, depict hunts, myths, daily life, and serving as a cultural memory and institution. But the cave paintings are also repetitive, mirroring the autoregressive nature of music and drumming.

As humans mastered the ability to produce speech, storytelling also evolved from cave paintings ... to oral traditions, such as Homer's epic poems, *The Iliad* and *The Odyssey,* shared by storytellers throughout the Bronze and Iron Ages. This oral tradition—stories passed down through spoken word, song, and chant across generations—was universal across earth's many and varied cultures and was used to preserve history, beliefs, and morals.

In Western Culture, storytelling became refined during the Hellenic period—1000 to 100 BCE. Aristotle's *Poetics* (335 BCE) began to formalize storytelling structure, while Aesop's *Fables* added morals to the oral tradition. Around the 6th century BCE plays came about as part of religious festivals honoring Dionysus, evolving from choral chants into structured performances. Storytellers such as Aristophanes, Aeschylus and Euripides formalized tragedy into the art form we know today.

In the Middle Ages and Renaissance (500-1600 CE) professional storytellers, known as bards in Europe, traveled from city to city, village to village, and even from farm to farm to continue oral traditions, weaving complex epics and histories to the delight of listeners.

Figure 53: Gutenberg Bible, Lenox copy. Picture by NYC Wanderer (Kevin Eng) in Wikimedia Commons

Meanwhile, at the end of this age, Gutenberg's movable type (c. 1440s) made books accessible, revolutionizing written storytelling. Books became plentiful. The Bible was printed and distributed throughout Europe.

The printing of the Bible marked a watershed moment in human communication—not merely because sacred text became democratized, but because the technology of mass printing itself unleashed something profound in the collective imagination. Within decades, a golden age of storytelling emerged that would have seemed impossible during the manuscript era. Shakespeare's Globe Theatre drew thousands to witness the full spectrum of human experience. The novel arose as a literary form, allowing consciousness to explore interior landscapes across hundreds of pages. Short stories compressed entire worlds into brief encounters. And eventually, science fiction emerged —perhaps the most significant mythmaking tradition of the modern age, allowing humanity to rehearse possible futures and alien encounters before they arrived.

Figure 54: William Shakespeare by John Taylor at the National Portrait Gallery London

Each innovation in communication technology, from movable type and the printing press to mass-market paperbacks, seemed to catalyze new forms of storytelling, as if the medium itself was preparing humanity for increasingly complex narratives about its place in the cosmos. The question we must ask is whether these weren't simply human innovations, but rather orchestrated developments in a much longer educational process—one designed to expand our capacity to comprehend what we might eventually encounter.

If Jacques Vallée is right about the Control System—that non-human intelligence has been guiding human consciousness through carefully timed events—then maybe this wasn't just human creativity at work. Maybe these storytelling breakthroughs were preparing us, step by step, to understand something we'd eventually need to face.

* * *

In the early twenty-first century, humanity created a new form of nonhuman intelligence: artificial intelligence systems capable of language. In the beginning, these systems—Large Language Models— did not speak and they did not hear. And yet they operated on precisely the same underlying architecture as natural human language. They predicted the next word based on the words that came before. Their language was not vocal but written.

Still, LLMs are built on the same sequential, rule-governed structure that emerged tens of thousands of years ago when humans first learned to speak.

Figure 55: Image of LLM Data Center

No other nonhuman intelligence—biological or artificial—has ever demonstrated this capacity. Except, perhaps, one.

Viewed in this light, the events at Church Creek take on a different character. The vocalizations recorded there may not be attempts at dialogue. They may not be messages in any conventional sense. Instead, they appear to point backward—toward the origin point of shared meaning itself. As if the presence encountered there was saying, *listen not to what we are saying* but *look at how language began*.

If interaction between intelligences requires a shared structure, then natural language may have been the necessary bridge all along. Not merely a human invention, but a medium—one that allowed something else to meet us halfway.

And if that is true, then the sounds heard and recorded by the team at Church Creek were neither random … symbolic … nor accidental.

They were reminding us where communication began—and what had to exist before any conversation could ever take place in a form that is essentially what it means to be human.

Seen through this long historical lens, the events at Church Creek acquire a different weight. The vowel-rich vocalizations, the structured chatter, the emphasis on sound over meaning—these do not resemble modern speech. They resemble something far older. They echo a time before writing. Before grammar. Before language became about information rather than connection.

If writing externalized language and artificial intelligence abstracted it further still, then the sounds heard at Church Creek point in the opposite direction—back toward origin. Back toward the moment when language was not yet a tool, but a bridge. But a bridge to what?

8

THE GRAND EXPERIMENT PART ONE

In August 2025, Dr. Jacques Vallée delivered a significant presentation at the Sol Forum entitled *UAP Encounters, Patterns, and the Signals of Intelligence*. Shortly after, his full talk was made available on YouTube.

A central point of Vallée's address was his Control System Hypothesis, which posits the existence of an ancient, guiding presence that may have steered humanity's development, perhaps even influencing the very emergence of language.

This hypothesis proposes that Unidentified Aerial Phenomena (UAP) encounters, Bigfoot sightings, and other related 'high-strangeness' phenomena are not merely random events or simple visitations. Instead, they are viewed as elements of a long-term, interactive process designed to shape human belief, culture, and cognition.

The intelligence behind this process, Vallée argues, does not reveal itself directly. It operates through ambiguity, symbolism, and patterns, subtly nudging humanity forward while meticulously preserving the mystery. In this view, the phenomenon acts less like a clear message and more like a feedback system. This system has, over millennia, repeatedly influenced human development—from the formation of myth and religion to technological advancements and, potentially, the initial appearance of language itself.

For Ron Meyer, after a decade of producing films and series about the Bigfoot phenomenon, Vallée's hypothesis was an epiphany. For the first time, he found a unifying framework capable of explaining the deeply paranormal nature of the Bigfoot phenomenon he had been studying, while also encompassing all other high-strangeness reports.

The Control System suggested that these encounters were not isolated anomalies, but coherent expressions of a single, underlying intelligence shaping human experience.

This realization clarified Ron's path: perhaps his film projects had been leading him toward a direct test of Vallée's idea. He recognized he could design a focused experiment—one built upon intention and interaction—and that the Church Creek site was the ideal location to carry it out.

Figure 56a: Dmitriy Rozin and Ron Meyer

So Ron decided to take a group of people to the Church Creek site on September 6, 2025. The idea was simple: repeat the same meditation and AEIOU chant protocol that had been implemented in Oklahoma and see if the presence would once again respond. The team called it the Close Encounters of the Sixth Kind, or CE-6 protocol.

The plan was to meet at Alan and Anna's house before heading into the mountains. The first to arrive was Jesse Morgan. He was followed by Ron and a friend from his martial arts training days, Dmitriy Rozin —a high-tech engineer and scientist specializing in the rapidly emerging world of artificial intelligence.

Dmitriy had never had any interest in Bigfoot, nor had he ever participated in a paranormal field investigation. Yet from his early years growing up in the Soviet Union, he was familiar with the idea that forests were places of unseen intelligence—places where folklore, fear, and mystery still lingered just beneath the surface.

Next to arrive were Gail Fowler, a modern-day shaman, and intuitive Dani Dodd. Both were long-time Bigfoot experiencers who described themselves as sensitives. While most of the group focused on investigating the Bigfoot phenomenon through observation and documentation, Dani and Gail practiced something altogether different: calling forth a felt presence.

Figure 56b: Dani Dodd and Gail Fowler

For them, Bigfoot was not something merely to be found, but something to be encountered—an intelligence that could be sensed, engaged, and communicated with directly. They were both members of an organization known as *The People of the Forest*, a loosely connected network of individuals who believe that meaningful interaction begins not with cameras or instruments, but openness and intention.

Their primary method was a practice known as toning, used to bring forth the presence of Bigfoot. In various healing and spiritual traditions—particularly within Native American cultures and modern intuitive communities—toning is a vocal technique intended to balance energy, release emotional blockages, and promote healing. Unlike singing, which emphasizes melody and performance, toning focuses on resonance—the vibration of sound as it moves through the body and outward into the surrounding environment.

Joining the team next was Paul Lee, who had served as the cameraman during the Oklahoma experience. The group carpooled to the Church Creek site, and waiting for them there was Kenny Collins —known to many in the region as 'Mr. Bigfoot of the Rockies.'

Almost immediately upon arrival, Dani and Gail began feeling the site's unusual energy.

"We're definitely being pulled out of our bodies," Gail said.

"We both have this kind of twitch," Dani added. "Part of that is sensing a shift in the energy here. It's not that we're going crazy—we're just feeling what the site is doing."

While the rest of the group began setting up chairs and forming a meditation circle, Alan took Paul and headed down toward the creek and tree line to deploy his new multi-microphone recording system. The area had been chosen deliberately, near a previous gifting site where earlier anomalies had been documented.

As Alan made his way to set up the audio recorder, three noteworthy events occurred. The first was the presence of a series of strange, uniform mounds clustered near the former gifting site. Alan stopped and his eyes narrowed, clearly puzzled. "These were not here last time."

At first glance, the formations appeared deliberate. Later, research revealed a natural explanation: northern pocket gopher mounds. These small rodents are capable of pushing soil to the surface while tunneling underground, leaving behind surprisingly symmetrical piles.

The second event was far more difficult to dismiss: two sharp, startling wood knocks echoed from the tree line. Alan pointed toward the forest. His breathing became more deliberate, and his voice quieted to a whisper. "There's something in the woods right there."

And then came the third event. As Alan continued setting up his recording equipment, a clear, unmistakable whoop rang out, captured on the camera audio. What was recorded fell into two distinct Bigfoot sound classes: percussive wood knocks and whoop-like vocalizations. The pairing of knock and whoop has been frequently documented in Bigfoot-related field reports across North America.

From that point on, Alan's sophisticated recording gear would continue rolling to the end of the grand experiment.

It was an intriguing and exciting beginning to the team's CE-6 protocol event: an attempt to make contact with the ancient presence.

Figure 57: Map of Church Creek with Meditation Circle

As dusk fell, all nine participants joined together and formed a circle. The purpose was to use the AEIOU chant to build a unified mental field. Two cameras rolled: one locked down north of the group pointing at the Church Creek tree line, the other handheld by Anna. Silence settled in, and Ron introduced the protocol's first step. As the process unfolded, everyone followed his simple instructions.

"Right, now we're going to do a simple mindfulness meditation followed by a chant to get us all in sync as one mind, as it were. So, close your eyes. Begin to sense any kind of movement, temperature, feelings in your body … They all make their appearance in something I call the Big Space. Others will say they appear in consciousness as experiences. The feelings could be an itch, the pressure of your butt in contact with the chair, or your feet on the ground. Notice how this becomes a cloud of sensations."

Figure 58: The group gathered for the CE-6 meditation/chant protocol

The group sat quietly and motionless for about thirty seconds, letting each person focus on their bodies. Then he continued.

"If you feel the need to scratch an itch, that's okay. Just focus on the sensations connected with your body. You might remember that you have had many sensations in your body and none of them, whether pleasant or painful, have remained. Everything is always flowing. It's good to remember that if you had a pain, it's all gone now."

Following his soft-spoken instructions, the group sat quietly for about a minute.

Ron spoke again, going on to the next step in the CE-6 protocol. "Now we're going to do a very primitive chant made up of the five vowels that form the basis of all spoken languages. They are A … E …

I ... O ... U, and we will do this five times together." Glancing at each member of the group, he asked, "Are we ready?"

When the chant concluded, the group rested quietly for a minute. Then Ron asked, "Does anybody want to say anything that occurred for them?"

Eyes closed, Alan was the first to respond. "There were many large wood-knock-like sounds that were behind us in the woods by the tree line."

"Yeah," Jesse confirmed.

Alan, with eyes still closed, continued. "Not to get too weird, but when I close my eyes, I have a thing where I can't see anything in my mind's eye. I can't visualize anything. I've never been able to do that. I can have dreams, but I can't actually close my eyes and see anything. Except right now." He opened his eyes and declared to the group, "But today when I closed my eyes, it was like there was a neutral density on my eyes. It was very muted, but it was the forest floor and it was constantly moving the entire time I had my eyes closed. And I've never experienced anything like that before. I don't know what it means."

Ron pointed to Gail. "Gail, are you nodding?"

She answered, "It's the same energy as we've been feeling. Bigfoot is here too."

Alan said, "I got the sense that it was here, also."

Anna, nodding affirmatively to her husband, said, "Earlier you said that, and I felt that too."

Ron motioned to Dani.

"Gail was saying it's like we are drunk. The energy is energetically drunk. I felt the ground moving."

Kenny spoke for the first time. "When I was in my car earlier, I thought it was running but it wasn't. I could feel this—like an underground vibration—just now in my body."

"So, for us, well for me especially," Gail said, "I feel waves. It's interesting how you say it feels like the idling of a car. So, the same thing. Welcome to our world!"

Laughing, Dani added, "I almost couldn't open my eyes."

"I had to force my eyes open. Even then it took a minute," Alan agreed.

Gail said excitedly, "They're ready for us."

Dmitriy made a wavelike gesture. "I definitely could feel the waves. The waves went through me."

The mindfulness meditation directed attention inward, toward the body itself—and that is exactly where the response appeared. Each person felt waves of energy in their own distinct way, as though something was answering the intention directly. How that connection occurred remains difficult to explain, but its presence was undeniable.

Figure 59: Jesse Morgan pointing to his ear indicating percussive sound

Back in the studio, Ron and Paul Lee reviewed the footage carefully. During the meditation and chant, eleven distinct percussive sounds were captured—each one recorded simultaneously on multiple camera microphones. Subsequent audio analysis revealed something surprising: the sounds did not match the acoustic signature of wood striking wood, nor that of branches breaking naturally.

One of the cameras had been locked down for the duration of the session, deliberately left without a human operator to eliminate the possibility of accidental contact with the microphone.

One moment stood out. While the group sat completely still, two sharp percussive strikes were heard in quick succession. On the footage, Jesse could be seen reacting immediately by pointing to his ear, confirming the sound was not an artifact added later, but something perceived in real time.

Then came the most striking event of all—four loud, rhythmic percussive sounds occurring in just over a single second. The cadence was unmistakable. Frame by frame, the footage told the same story: every participant remained perfectly still.

Figure 60: Alan Megargle beating his chest, replicating the rhythmic percussive sound

In the studio, the audio engineer isolated the sequence and played it back for Alan. As a musician, he heard something others might not.

"What's interesting is that it's rhythmic. You can hear a beat to it. It has a clapping quality to it." Demonstrating by striking his chest with both hands, Alan said, "It sounds like a chest beat. Like a great ape beating its chest."

Canting his head and carefully listening again, Alan added, "That's what it sounds like to me. Possibly like a Bigfoot beating its chest."

If so, the implication was profound. The response was not linguistic in any modern sense. It pointed toward something far older than words. Long before language, there was rhythm. Before meaning, there was cadence. Music, in its simplest form, may have preceded spoken language—sharing the same auto-regressive architecture that later evolved into speech.

Back at the Church Creek site, the group prepared for the next CE-6 session, as the presence was about to express itself through the Bigfoot phenomenon in a way that would deepen the mystery and amplify a sense of wonder that was both unexpected and profoundly exciting.

9

MUSIC AS THE PROTO-LANGUAGE AND SOCIAL GLUE

G reat storytelling hasn't changed since our earliest human ancestors returned from a hunt to tell their fellow tribe members the harrowing tale of killing a gigantic mammoth and how they had to protect their kill from sabretooth tigers. The hunting party's leader, let's call him Dävê, had no words except for a few glottal stops and grunts. Yes, human anatomy of the throat, mouth and ear had evolved to where sounds could be made and heard, but Dävê had no words yet. Still, he had to tell the others of his clan the harrowing story so that the knowledge of how he and his team survived the kill and the attack by the great cats could be passed on to others. So how did he tell the tale?

Figure 61: Charles Robert Knight Mural - Wikimedia Commons

The most probable answer is drumming.

The simplest rhythmic beating—the clapping of hands or the striking of wood—is believed by many researchers to be what came before spoken language. The oldest form of human communication, drumming creates its own meaning and momentum through rhythm and repetition.

Alan demonstrated this type of possible communication from the presence or phenomenon by beating his chest to the rhythm recorded during the CE-6 meditation/chant protocol as referenced in chapter 8— The Grand Experiment Part One.

Figure 62: Alan Megargle beating his chest

Picture this scene: Dävê sits beside the large communal fire, flames roaring skyward, pushing back the dark night. The clan elders sit patiently. The smallest children are fidgeting, eyes wide open, eagerly waiting for the story to begin. Dävê picks up two pieces of wood and starts beating on a log. At first, the rhythm is strong and steady. Each strike tells of the patient stalk by the hunters as they trail the giant mammoth. The beats become faster, louder as Dävê tells the story of how the hunters rushed forward and hurled their spears, the razor sharp stone spearheads piercing the tough mammoth hide, injuring vital organs. Finally, the beast dies.

The tone of the story now shifts. The drum beats out the grave tones of staving off starvation in solid slow whacks. With stone axes the hunters peel away the hide to get at the flesh underneath. The kill will feed the clan for the next few winter months. The hide will go to make clothes and tents. The sinew will be used for thread to make clothes. Bones will form charms and amulets and fishhooks.

Figure 63: Drumming with a group - Dr. Ondřej Havelka; Wikimedia Commons

Once more the drumbeat changes, becomes more intense, more frantic. A sabretooth tiger appears. Dävê's drumming interpretation of the tale becomes frenzied. The fear the hunters feel at the approach of this most dangerous predator fills the night. The bleak sounds seem almost to overpower the raging fire itself. But Dävê's next strikes tell of the courage of a young hunter whose spear pierces the tiger's eye and drops the great predator as it rushes forward.

It is a fascinating story retold across thousands of campfires hundreds of thousands of years ago. And it reveals something profound about how human communication began.

The Pattern That Built Language

Music, just like natural language and physical reality, is fundamentally autoregressive.[1]

It works by building one moment on top of the last. Think of it like dominoes falling in sequence.

The drumming story of paleolithic hunters shows us this perfectly. Each new sound, each new phrase, each new beat comes from the pattern established just before. Every musical tradition, from a bone flute carved thirty thousand years ago to a modern electronic dance track, relies on this same principle. And drumming is the father of all music.

Before humans could speak a sentence, they could tap out a beat together. This shared rhythmic structure provided the foundation for organizing thoughts and sounds into meaningful language. Music's rhythmic structure, its meter and tempo, mirror the underlying patterns needed for humans to produce complex languages. Both rhythm and language rely on recognizing patterns, anticipating what comes next, and noticing when something breaks the pattern.

Drumming did something else critical for human evolution. It created group unity through shared experience. The primary function of early music was not entertainment but social bonding. When people drum, chant, and dance together, they must move in harmony and sync up with each other. On a physical level, group dancing triggers the release of oxytocin and endorphins in the body. These are the same hormones released during bonding experiences like hugging, laughter, or sex. They foster deep trust, reduce stress, and blur individual identity into group identity. These shared, non-verbal emotional experiences were necessary to form large, stable social groups. And large, stable social groups were required for complex spoken languages to emerge.

---

1. Autoregressive means that each new step is created by referencing what came immediately before it. Instead of seeing or determining an entire sequence all at once, an autoregressive process unfolds gradually, building the present moment from its own past.

From simple hand-claps, music immediately began a journey of constant innovation. It never settled for a single form. It continuously created new styles, instruments, and structures, moving from drumming and more complex instruments to human vocalizations such as chanting and eventually to songs.

Drumming, chants and songs were also the original memory tools. They helped people memorize essential survival information like hunting techniques, migration routes, which plants were edible, and the laws of the clan. These rhythmic patterns ensured the reliable transmission of vital knowledge across generations, a function later inherited by language itself.

Over the last two hundred thousand years, music has evolved from ancient forms based on rhythm and natural sounds to the complex, modern genres we know today. This evolution happened through cultural exchange and technological advancements in instruments, musical notation, and recording technology. Over time, this led to the creation of entirely new styles, the blending of genres, and massive changes in how music is produced, consumed, and distributed.

The Mystery Behind the Music

But what if there's something deeper at work? What if music wasn't just a human invention?

If Jacques Vallée's Control System hypothesis is right—that an ancient non-human intelligence has been nudging humanity forward through experiences of mystery—then music may have been one of its earliest levers for shaping humanity's uniqueness.

Paleolithic humans reported hearing voices in the wind, rhythmic stones, and unexplainable tonal phenomena deep in caves. These acoustic anomalies—echoes, resonance chambers, infrasonic pulses that you feel more than hear—may have been early encounters with a guiding presence. Caves like Lascaux and Chauvet, famous for their ancient paintings, show evidence that artwork was placed exactly where sound resonance peaks occurred. These weren't random locations. Our ancestors were painting in spots where sound behaved strangely, where the cave itself seemed to amplify and transform noise into something otherworldly.

The implication is striking: people did not just see the mystery. They heard it.

Imagine you're a human living thirty thousand years ago. You venture deep into a sacred cave, beyond where sunlight reaches. In the flickering light of your torch, you begin to chant or beat a drum. Suddenly, the cave responds. Your voice comes back to you transformed, deeper, resonating in ways that make your chest vibrate. Sounds seem to come from everywhere and nowhere. You're hearing something that feels alive, intelligent, responsive.

What would you conclude? That the spirits were speaking back to you? That the gods inhabited this place? That you had crossed a threshold into another realm?

The presence, whatever it is, may have used these acoustic anomalies to shift human consciousness toward abstraction, ritual, and symbolism. These experiences laid the groundwork for complex culture, for religion, for art, for the belief that there's more to reality than what we can see and touch.

This pattern of rhythmic communication persists into modern encounters. Remember the team's experience at Church Creek during the AEIOU meditation protocol? The unseen presence produced a distinct rhythmic sequence in response to the chanting. It wasn't random noise or natural forest sounds. It was a patterned beat using the same structure that underlies both music and language. Alan, who is a musician, imagined it as a Bigfoot or guerrilla slapping its chest in a deliberate rhythm. The phenomenon was prompting us by communicating in a rhythm pattern, just as it may have done tens of thousands of years ago. It was using music's autoregressive architecture to bridge the gap between natural language today and something from the ancient past.

Gifts From the Gods

Later in Paleolithic culture, more sophisticated instruments were introduced—drums with animal hide stretched across frames, bone flutes carved with precise holes, bull roarers that created eerie wailing sounds when spun overhead. Many cultures describe these instruments as gifts from the gods, ancestors, or beings from the sky. The Aboriginal people of Australia say the didgeridoo was given to them by the Rainbow Serpent. Native American traditions speak of the first drums being created by spirits or animal helpers. Ancient Chinese legends credit the invention of musical instruments to divine or semi-divine figures.

In Vallée's model, such myths may not be pure fiction. They could be artifacts of a genuine interaction with a phenomenon teaching humans to perceive and create structured sound. The 'gods' who gave humanity music might have been something far stranger than imagined deities—perhaps the same intelligence that leaves footprints in remote forests and responds to vowel chants with rhythmic patterns.

Mystery drives innovation, and music is one of its primary tools. Ancient civilizations from Sumer and Egypt to India and Greece discovered that music reflects the structure of the universe itself. The ancient Greek mathematician Pythagoras spoke of the music of the spheres, claiming that planets and stars generate harmonies as they move through space. The Vedas, ancient Hindu texts, describe sound as the first emanation of creation, the original vibration from which all existence springs. Egyptians built ceremonial chambers in their pyramids and temples tuned to specific resonant frequencies, designed to alter consciousness during rituals.

Under Vallée's hypothesis, this is not coincidence. The presence uses harmonic mystery to nudge humanity toward mathematics, astronomy, architecture, and philosophy. By experiencing the strange acoustic properties of sacred spaces, by discovering mathematical ratios in musical intervals, by feeling their consciousness shift during ceremonial music, our ancestors were being guided toward new ways of thinking about reality.

The presence's influence using music does not stop in antiquity but continues throughout history to the present day. From the Hellenic Age through the medieval period and into the Renaissance, music became a tool for healing, worship, mathematics and altered states of consciousness. Gregorian chants, designed to be performed in stone cathedrals with long reverberation times, create a wash of overlapping tones that dissolve individual voices into a collective sound. Sufi music uses repetitive spinning and chanting to induce trance states. Jewish cantillation transforms scripture into melodic recitation. Tibetan throat singing produces multiple pitches simultaneously from a single voice, creating harmonics that seem physically impossible.

All of these traditions aim at the same goal: to tune consciousness to something beyond ordinary perception. And here's the remarkable thing—mystical encounters, experiences of the divine or otherworldly, happen most frequently in musical contexts. People report seeing visions during drumming ceremonies, feeling the presence of spirits during chanting, encountering something transcendent during deep meditation accompanied by sacred music.

In Vallée's framing, the Control System escalates the mystery signal through music, pushing human minds toward deeper metaphysical inquiry. The stranger the music, the more it breaks from everyday experience, the more it opens doors to alternative states of consciousness.

While the Renaissance was a golden age in the arts, what followed was a breakthrough across all levels of human interest, from the arts and science to philosophy; something was accelerating.

* * *

Over the next four hundred years, Western music became increasingly complex. Composers developed multiple harmonies weaving in and out of each other, created large orchestras with dozens of instruments playing coordinated parts, and used mathematical composition techniques. As science grew and expanded its understanding of the physical world, music became more structured, more computational, more rule-based. Humanity was being guided toward a new kind of intelligence—logical, predictive, algorithmic.

Interestingly, if not somewhat unsettling, some philosophers believe that music has acted as a rehearsal for artificial intelligence. Think about what music requires: pattern recognition, prediction of what comes next, the ability to generate novel variations on established themes, and the capacity to produce something that follows rules while still being creative. These are exactly the capabilities that define modern AI systems.

The twentieth and twenty-first centuries strongly support this idea.

In the twentieth century, Vallée's idea of presence and mystery is validated by breakthroughs in technology—radio, television, satellites, and computers. As these technologies emerged, people began reporting strange signals over radio waves, unintelligible voices in static, unexplained harmonics in broadcasts, and anomalous transmissions that seemed to come from nowhere. Music and mystery merged again and again throughout the century.

Some avant garde classical composers described receiving inspiration from other intelligences, from sources beyond their conscious minds. The same phenomenon appears in pop music. Icons like John Lennon and Bruce Springsteen have reported that songs emerged out of nowhere in an instant, fully formed, and all they had to do was write them down. Lennon described it as tuning into a radio station that was always broadcasting. Springsteen spoke of songs arriving like gifts from somewhere else.

Once again we can see how music drives innovation. And we can see how the presence may be pushing humanity toward the twenty-first century's digital consciousness, preparing us for the age of artificial intelligence.

Today's AI Large Language Models are fundamentally built on the same principle as early human music. They generate the next element based on patterns established just before. The same structure that governed the first ritual chant now governs Open AI's ChatGPT, Anthropic's Claude, and Google's Gemini in generating music, art, and writing. The original stories told with drums at a raging campfire are now amplified through algorithms that work on music's autoregressive nature.

* * *

During the AEIOU meditation protocol at Church Creek, the phenomenon responded with eleven percussive sounds, including four distinct rhythmic beats, while simultaneously, during the collective meditation and chanting, every participant felt waves of energy pulsing through their bodies. This dual response—rhythmic percussion combined with physical sensations—mirrors exactly what happened when our paleolithic ancestors drummed and chanted together around campfires. Just as those ancient rhythms triggered the release of bonding hormones and synchronized the bodies of early humans into cohesive groups, the Church Creek phenomenon used the same mechanism: rhythm and shared physical sensation to create unity among participants. The phenomenon responded to the team with humanity's oldest form of communication—the beat—while generating the same unifying bodily experience that originally bound human tribes together and laid the groundwork for complex language to emerge.

Whatever this intelligence is, it speaks a language older than words. It communicates through rhythm, through sound, through the same fundamental patterns that gave birth to human consciousness, human culture, and human language. And now, as we stand on the threshold of artificial intelligence and digital consciousness, those same patterns are emerging in our technology.

The question is no longer whether something has been guiding human evolution through music and mystery. The evidence suggests something has. The question now is where this guidance is leading us, and whether we're ready for what comes next when the beat changes once again.

10

SECOND EXPERIMENT

When the first CE-6 protocol had been completed, the team prepared for a second session. In anticipation of what the next session might bring, Alan Megargle walked to his vehicle to gather a full array of high-tech equipment that would be deployed for the remainder of the investigation.

"I decided to bring everything," Alan explained. "All the electronics and gadgets to the Church Creek site. The REM-Pod, the spirit box, along with a 360-degree camera, digital telescope, handheld FLIR unit, sky camera mounted on my vehicle, and the Tesla coil. I wanted to see what kinds of responses we might get."

From that point on, cameraman Paul Lee would film continuously throughout the night. Anna Megargle, working with the second camera, moved selectively, choosing moments she felt were significant. Jesse Morgan took charge of the night-vision camera. The idea behind employing the vast array of technical gear was simple: cast as wide a technological net as possible and see what—if anything—responded.

What the team did not know at the time was that from this point forward, the presence would express itself through a sequence of events that affected everyone there, though the effects would not be recognized until later in the edit suite, when Ron and Paul reviewed the audio captured by the microphones Alan had earlier placed near Church Creek.

However, the event that would have the greatest impact on Ron occurred while the group chatted amongst themselves, waiting for the second meditation and AEIOU chant to begin. From the wooded area northwest of the circle, a male voice emerged—disembodied, yet unmistakable—speaking Ron's name.

Ron remembers being startled, genuinely confused, and instinctively replying, "Yes?"

Alan turned to Jesse. "Did you call Ron?"

"No," Jesse replied.

Figure 64a: Paul Lee filming meditation group

Figure 64b: Jesse Morgan with his night vision camera

Alan paused, then said aloud, "He just said yes to someone saying his name."

Anna looked toward the northwest trees and pointed. "I heard it," she said. "I thought somebody was over there."

"I heard it too," Dmitriy added.

"That was weird," Ron said, still trying to process what had just happened.

The moment lingered in the air. Ron, long familiar with ufologist John Keel's unsettling observation—*If you start studying paranormal phenomena, they begin studying you*—felt the weight of those words more acutely than ever.[1]

Later audio analysis in the studio proved inconclusive. The synchronized camera recordings, including the 360-degree camera raised twelve feet above the group, captured only a brief low-frequency consonant sound before Dani Dodd's voice, speaking to Gail Fowler, overwhelmed the rest. Post-processing and enhancement suggested a timbre closer to the beginning of *rɔn* or *ɹan* than to something like 'hey.' Once again, the presence had revealed itself only partially—never fully, never cleanly. Like a question half-answered, it left just enough evidence to confirm something had occurred, but not enough to define what that something was.

Ron decided not to use the occurrence in the documentary because the event would take too long to explain.

Afterward, Alan conducted a quick sweep of the surrounding area and sky with the FLIR unit. No unusual heat signatures appeared.

* * *

As full darkness settled over Church Creek, Ron began the second meditation and AEIOU chant. With Paul and Jesse filming, the group's focus shifted outward—listening intently for any fleeting sound, move-

---

1. John Keel wrote the parapsychology thriller, *The Mothman Prophecies* in 1972. The book relates Keel's accounts of his investigation into alleged sightings of a large, winged creature known as Mothman in the vicinity of Point Pleasant, West Virginia, during 1966 and 1967.

ment, or signal that might emerge from the surrounding forest. Hopefully, whatever had spoken here before would choose to speak again.

Ron's voice drifted calmly through the darkness as he repeated the same meditation/chant protocol from the first session, only this time the focus was on sounds. "Now become aware of any sounds," he said. "Notice how they, like feelings, come and go. Fleeting... though of course, you can still hear my voice."

Figure 65: Group in second meditation circle

Alan suddenly broke the stillness. "Did you hear that?" he said quietly. "They're vocalizing right behind you, Ron."

Gail confirmed it with a simple, unambiguous, "Yeah!"

Ron's back was turned toward the Church Creek tree line, indicating where the vocalizations were coming from. Alan was right. Something remarkable was happening.

During this session, eight distinct, chatter-like vocalizations were captured across multiple microphones. They were clear, rapid, and structured—proto-speech once again. The sounds closely resembled the so-called Sierra-type vocalizations long associated with Bigfoot— quick, syllabic bursts that felt uncannily conversational. Played one after another, they gave the impression that more than one entity was speaking, responding, or exchanging information. Moreover, the tone and timbre matched the Bigfoot chatter previously recorded at Church Creek. At the same time, no percussive sounds occurred during the session.

While the Samurai-style chatter was riveting, the most unusual sound of the night came just before the final AEIOU chant began. Several microphones picked up what initially sounded like an echo of the vowels—AEIOU. But it wasn't an echo.

Figure 66: Map of Church Creek with Meditation Circle

What the audio analysis revealed was something far stranger: a sound shaped by what must have been a living throat and mouth, producing a single, continuous tone that slowly changed form over time—almost as if something were attempting to vocalize A-E-I-O-U in one extended breath.

In the studio the vocalization opened with 'ah' or 'uh'… tightening into 'ee'… then dropping toward 'oh' and 'oo.' Just as importantly, cameraman Paul Lee, who doubles as a sound engineer, and Alan, agreed the continuous AEIOU sounds were not something a human voice could easily produce.

So, what was it?

The anomalous nature of the vocalization and its eerie, almost supernatural mimicking of human sounds suggested the Bigfoot presence was answering back in its own approximation of language—as if to say, *We are here.* Yet even in this moment of apparent communication, the phenomenon withheld clarity. The sound was intelligible enough to recognize as mimicry, but too strange to categorize. Once again, the mystery deepened rather than resolved.

Figure 67a: SLS Kinect Camera infrared grid projected across the Church Creek tree line

As soon as the meditation circle broke apart, Alan motioned to Dmitriy and headed toward the edge of Church Creek with his SLS Kinect camera. Paul followed the pair, filming their progress. At the same time, Ron, from the meditation circle, activated his green laser, sweeping it slowly across the area, hoping to energize the tree line. It was a technique he had learned during the investigation at Bradshaw Ranch. Some researchers speculate that when the beam ionizes the molecules it passes through, it provides a source of energy for entities to materialize.

An SLS (Structured Light Sensor) Kinect camera projects a structured grid of infrared light into the surrounding space. When something disrupts that grid, the system attempts to reconstruct the disturbance as a three-dimensional form. Originally designed for video game motion-sensing technology, the device has since found an unlikely second life in paranormal investigation—where it has been used to reveal what some describe as unseen presences: humanlike figures appearing where no physical body can be seen. Ron and his investigative team had successfully used the SLS Kinect camera at Bradshaw Ranch to trace the form of an entity interacting with the Tesla coil.

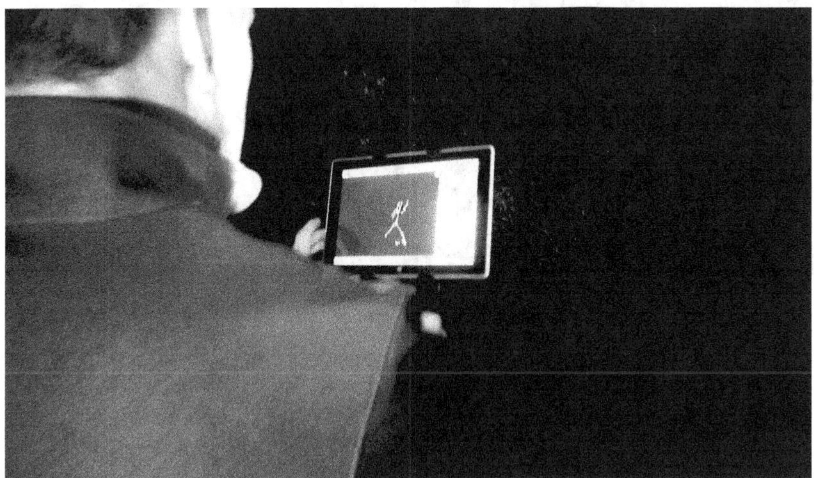

Figure 67b: Human-like figure on the SLS Kinect camera screen

The hope at Church Creek was to detect a possible Bigfoot manifestation in the same area where an unexplained light phenomenon had been recorded months earlier.

Dmitriy led the way down toward the tree line, sweeping his flashlight ahead of them. Alan followed closely, struggling with the awkward SLS Kinect camera in one hand while trying to operate its controls with the other.

When they reached the edge of the forest, Alan began slowly scanning along the tree line when, without warning, he froze. "Hold on—I got it."

For a brief moment, a humanlike figure appeared on the SLS screen.

"Did you see that, Paul?" Alan asked urgently. "Did you get it with your camera?"

"I did," Paul replied.

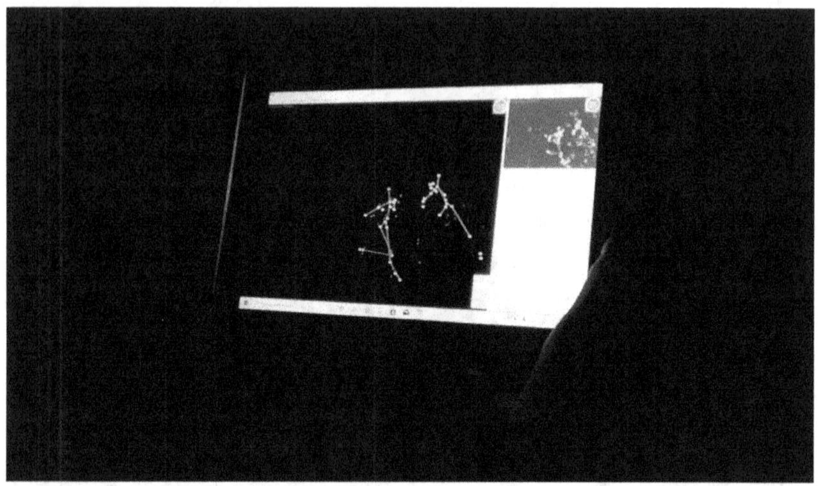

Figure 68: Two entities on the SLS Kinect camera screen

"I don't think I hit record fast enough on the SLS," Alan said, frustration creeping into his voice. Then, more animated now, he turned to Dmitriy. "It was there. Did you see it?"

"I saw it," Dmitriy said. "I saw it! I saw it!"

The SLS Kinect camera was still rolling when, suddenly, another humanlike figure materialized on the screen. Calm but focused, Alan spoke directly to it. "We can see you. Can you crouch?"

The figure crouched.

"You can," Alan said quietly. After a brief pause, he added, "I've got to stop recording for a second." Paul's camera, however, never stopped rolling.

Ron continued to sweep the area with his green laser, bathing the trees and creek bank in a thin, luminous light.

Suddenly, the entity was back on the SLS display. This time a second entity joined it.

"Now we've got two," Alan whispered to the others.

Almost immediately, the second figure vanished, and in the next instant both were gone.

The humanlike figures appearing on the screen seemed impossible to explain. Were they a manifestation of Bigfoot? Or yet another fleeting glimpse into the deeper mystery that seemed to hover over the Church Creek site? The figures appeared and disappeared with a timing that felt deliberate—as if offering just enough to maintain interest without providing definitive proof.

Whatever the figures were, the experience had a profound effect on Dmitriy, who began weaving back and forth unsteadily, as if struggling to remain upright. "I didn't feel anything before," he said, his voice trembling. "Earlier it was just waves. But now it's like I'm shaking completely. My whole body is shaking. I can't stand still." He paused, trying to steady himself. "It's like the energy is pulsating through me."

* * *

While Alan and Dmitriy were making brief contact with the anomalous figures near the tree line, something else occurred back at the meditation circle. A sudden, unmistakable odor permeated the space.

Anna wrinkled her nose and whispered, "Maybe the Bigfoot has come."

"So, they smell different too," Dani said. "Like… sometimes kind of strange."

Gail, eyes closed, seemed to sense the source immediately. "It's down at the site," she said, indicating the creek. "Not up here."

Ron noticed it next. Then Kenny.

"It smells like the Bigfoot that once came for me," Dani said. "It smelled like a campfire."

Anna froze, a realization flashing across her face as she recognized the smell from a previous encounter. "Jesse. Did you hear that?" she asked, then caught herself. "I mean—did you smell that?"

Figure 69: Dani Dodd smelling foul odor

"The Sasquatch kind of comes in and they smell like campfire," Dani said.

"Do you remember?" Anna asked Jesse Morgan.

Jesse, who had been with Anna during their first nocturnal investigation at Church Creek two months earlier, did. It was the very same scent Jesse and Anna had encountered—just moments before recording what they believed to be Bigfoot chatter at the Church Creek site. "It smelled like campfire," Jesse said, "but it had a hint of something else."

"It's like—you know when something is off, but not wrong?" Dani added. "Kind of like that."

"Yeah," Jesse said.

"But mixed in with the campfire smell," Dani continued. "Like it's in there."

"That's the closest I can come," Jesse said. "But for me, there was definitely something else in it."

"Like an undertone," Gail offered.

"Yeah," Jesse agreed.

"You've got to pay attention to your noses too!" Dani said.

Whatever the presence at Church Creek was, it seemed to reveal itself in layers—first feelings, then sound, and now even scent—each one offering a clue while refusing to resolve into anything fully known. The pattern was unmistakable: the phenomenon engaged the senses systematically, never all at once, always leaving room for doubt even as evidence accumulated.

Alan returned the SLS Kinect camera to his vehicle and retrieved the FLIR unit. As he scanned the sky above the Church Creek tree line, an unusual hotspot appeared on the thermal imaging camera's screen.

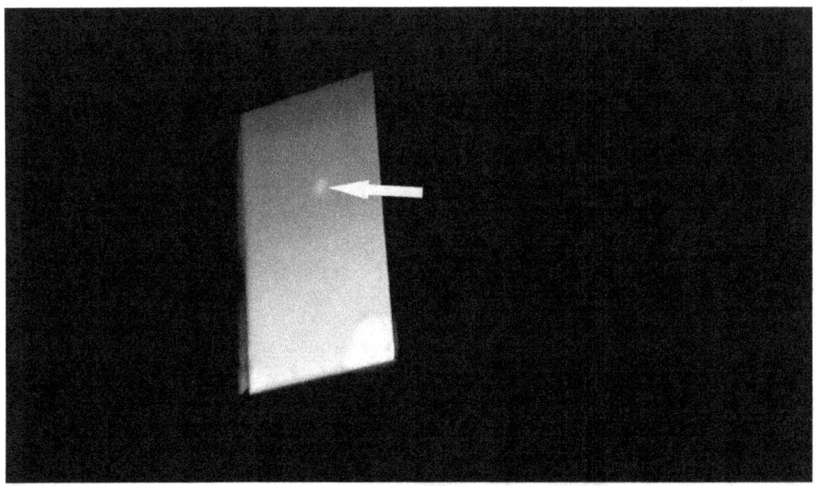

Figure 70: Image from the FLIR camera

"Can you film my screen?" Alan asked Ron, angling the device upward.

Ron studied the display. "Wow, that's like the UAPs at Skinwalker Ranch!"

"I don't think it's picking up a cloud," Alan said. "Would a cloud even be hot?"

Ron thought about it for a moment. "Yes," he said. "They can be warmer than the surrounding air."

The anomaly faded as quickly as it had appeared.

For a moment, excitement surged—another mystery unfolding in real time. But this one resolved into something ordinary. A natural phenomenon, a cloud.

Not everything at Church Creek resisted explanation.

But the next event did.

* * *

As Alan returned the FLIR unit to the vehicle, Dani and Gail began toning. They initiated the practice, asking for the felt energy of Bigfoot to reveal itself and connect with them. A long, rising tone of love was sent outward into the night, carried on breath and intention toward the presence they sensed nearby. Kenny felt compelled to join in, adding his voice to the sustained tone.

Figure 71: Dani Dodd and Gail Fowler toning

At that same moment, Jesse's night-vision camera captured something unexpected. Near the tree line, two pairs of small, steady lights appeared—positioned like eyes—holding their place in the darkness for nearly twenty seconds before Jesse ended the recording.

Across countless Bigfoot reports, the same pattern appears again and again: mysterious, glowing eyeshine emerging in the darkness in response to human focus, precise in its timing, yet stubbornly resistant to explanation. Was the appearance of the possible eyeshine during the toning a form of call and response—or merely a coincidence?

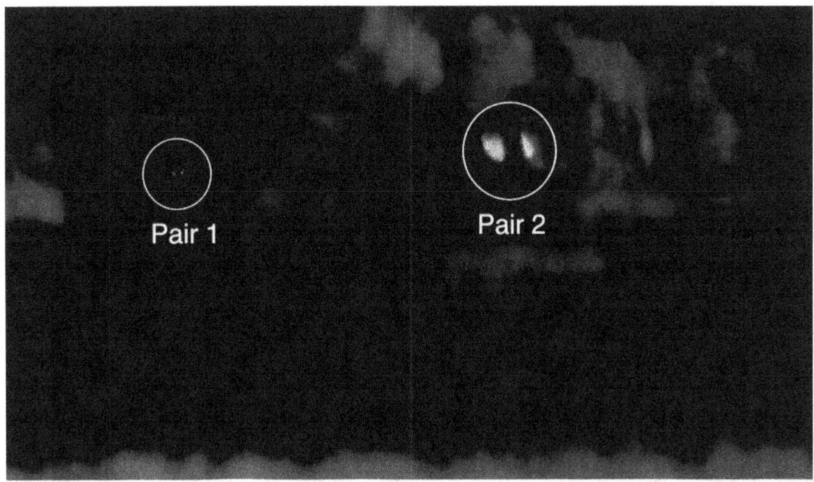

Figure 72: Image of the two pairs of reflected eyes

Weeks later, the team returned to the site to uncover the source of the two pairs of lights, searching carefully for reflective objects that might account for the infrared response. An old, battered sign was eventually located that could explain the nearer set of lights. But nothing accounted for the smaller pair farther back in the trees.

The event echoed an earlier occurrence from two months prior, when a single white light near the Church Creek tree line remained fixed on the night-vision camera as Alan walked to its apparent location. He stood right beside where the light should be. Incredibly, no physical source could be found, even as Anna continued filming through the night-vision camera.

Soon after the initial toning, everyone except Dmitriy moved down toward the Church Creek tree line. Following the SLS Kinect camera experience, he instead returned briefly to the meditation circle before walking alone into the nearby woods. Later, he described what happened there.

"I walked into the forest," he said, "and I felt like I was part of it. There was a lot of warmth and energy—pulsations moving through my body. It was absolutely unusual. I felt like I belonged there… like I was part of that place." He looked up, as if searching for the right words.

"No thoughts," he said. "Just the feelings." After a pause, he added one more thing. "There was no 'me.' No me, per se."

What Dmitriy described was strikingly familiar—a classic account of the non-dual experience reported by mystics, contemplatives, and meditators throughout history: a moment in which the sense of a separate self falls away, replaced by a direct feeling of unity with the world itself.

Figure 73: Dmitriy Rozin reporting his non-dual experience

Whether prompted by the environment, the collective ritual, or something more elusive, the experience left its mark. And like so much else at Church Creek, it offered no clear explanation—only the unmistakable sense that something had briefly shifted, both within and without.

As the rest of the group reached the Church Creek tree line, Ron quietly instructed Anna to focus her camera on Dani and Gail.

* * *

A full moon hung high above the tree line, its pale light penetrating the darkness. In its glow, the women appeared almost removed from the forest around them, their movements slow and deliberate, as if something unseen were passing through rather than simply surrounding them. On camera, the effect was striking—subtle shifts of posture, a softening of expression—suggesting an energy in motion, entering and moving through their bodies.

They began toning again, this time offering gratitude and love toward the Bigfoot presence they felt nearby. The sound rose into the trees, steady and unforced. Kenny joined in once more, his voice blending naturally with theirs.

When the toning ended, the sensitives described a distinct warmth, like being held—an embrace they attributed to the presence itself.

"It's okay," Gail said softly. "We can feel you. You don't have to come out." After a few deep breaths, she continued. "And thank you for taking care of the land, so that others may experience it too, surrounded by your love."

Kenny spoke next, directing his words into the darkness. "Your energy and love have changed my way of life. If it weren't for you, I'd either be dead or in jail."

"They're teachers too," Gail said quietly.

"Yeah," Kenny agreed. "Right now, we thank you for changing lives."

"I do thank you for letting us connect with you tonight," Gail added.

"And thank you for all the vocalizations we heard tonight," Kenny said.

Dani suddenly pointed toward the tree line. "A Bigfoot is crouching down. I keep seeing faces."

Gail gestured in the same direction. "There's a big male one. I feel his energy."

"He's in the middle," Dani said, nodding toward a specific tree. "By that one."

"I call him Alpha," Gail said.

Once more, the women and Kenny began to tone, their voices rising together beneath the moonlight, sending one final offering of sound into the trees—into whatever was listening.

Figure 74: Alan Megargle and Dani Dodd looking at the spot where they saw Bigfoot

At the same time the toning continued, Alan—thermal camera in hand—wandered off into the wooded area. It was something he often did, stepping away from the group to seek a more personal encounter with what he referred to simply as "the Bigfoot presence." He moved quietly through the trees, following the felt sense of something nearby rather than any clear visual cue.

When he returned, he was eager to compare notes. Emerging from the tree line, Alan called out, "Hey ladies—are you hearing anything down here?"

"Yeah," Gail replied. "A little bit. Like a crackle. Not exactly crackling…"

"I got it on the thermal," Alan said.

"Because you're seeing it between those trees, right?" Dani asked.

Alan reached the group, standing beside Dani, Gail, and Kenny. "Yeah. I wasn't sure at first if I wasn't watching one of you, because it wasn't moving on the thermal. Then I blinked a bit, and I saw it duck down."

"Yeah," Gail said quietly.

Alan pointed toward the same section of trees Dani had indicated earlier. "So, it was right in there."

"There's an alpha Bigfoot we toned to—Ace," Dani said. "He gave us his name. He's been back there, moving."

"Okay, that's cool," Alan said. "Because it was right over there next to that tree. Right in there." He pointed again, marking the spot.

"Yep," Dani said.

Jesse stepped in. He wanted to try a series of whoops before they left.

Everyone agreed.

Jesse called out five times into the darkness, the sounds carrying through the trees—one final attempt at contact before the night at Church Creek came to a close. But there was no reply.

* * *

Between the two sessions, Alan had placed two REM-Pods, a spirit box, and a Tesla coil in the center of the meditation circle.

A 360-degree camera was also erected there—mounted roughly twelve feet above the ground—recording continuously, its elevated perspective watching and listening over the meditation circle even when no one was nearby. However, it did record all the percussive sounds and chatter.

Throughout the rest of the night, the other devices remained silent. No alarms sounded. No lights were triggered. No unusual voices recorded on the spirit box. No obvious interaction with any of the equipment occurred.

As the investigation began wrapping up, Alan went down to the creek to gather his audio recorder. For reasons he could not fully explain, Kenny Collins felt the sudden impulse to take one of the REM-Pods from the meditation circle down to the Creek edge. Alan, watching his movements, told Paul to follow him with his camera.

Kenny placed the REM-Pod on the ground and then slowly backed away.

Immediately, it activated.

"Are you here?" Kenny asked softly. He stepped back farther. The device silenced. "Wow… thank you," Kenny said, visibly surprised. "Will you approach again?"

The REM-Pod activated once more.

Kenny stood perfectly still, amazement spreading across his face. "Thank you. We're not here to hurt you. Are you okay?"

The REM-Pod went silent again.

Kenny tried once more. "Are you here with us?"

Figure 75: Kenny Collins interacting with Bigfoot activating the REM-POD

The presence appeared to reenter the REM-Pod's radio-frequency field, activating it in response—an apparent yes.

Then silence returned.

At that moment, one of Jesse's howls cut through the night.

Kenny asked another question. "Do you like them doing that? Turn on if you don't."

The REM-Pod remained silent.

"Thank you," Kenny said simply.

He turned toward the camera, joy unmistakable on his face, and gave a thumbs-up. For Kenny, this moment represented the fulfillment of something lifelong—an experience of direct interaction with what he believed to be Bigfoot.

It was the only REM-Pod activation recorded at Church Creek since Richard Estep's first encounter months earlier.

Viewed through the lens of Jacques Vallée's Control System hypothesis, the event revealed a striking pattern. The presence had ignored the equipment when it sat in the meditation circle for hours, surrounded by cameras and witnesses. Only when Kenny—acting on impulse—moved the device to a new location, alone, at the moment of his deepest emotional investment, did it respond. The phenomenon was not random at all, but selective— engaging only at certain moments, under specific conditions, perhaps intentionally guiding the investigation over more than a year and a half. Each interaction deepened the mystery rather than resolving it, as if the phenomenon itself was less interested in being documented than in shaping those who sought to document it.

And yet, the final piece of evidence to emerge from this grand experiment had not revealed itself in the field. It surfaced later—back in the studio.

The first footage reviewed was Alan's sky camera that was mounted on the rooftop of his vehicle. Throughout the entire investigation, nothing unusual appeared—only the steady procession of commercial aircraft moving across the night sky.

But the most surprising discovery came from the audio. During playback, deep infrasound pulses were identified, captured simultaneously across multiple microphones. Each pulse lasted roughly half a second, and occurred seventeen times over a ninety-five-minute window. The first pulse appeared shortly after the initial meditation session, the final one just before all recording ceased.

No one had consciously heard them in real time.

These pulses were irregularly spaced, recorded simultaneously on five microphones spread over an area larger than a football field, and displayed a consistent frequency signature centered around twenty-three hertz. There were no people moving nearby, no machinery operating, no falling trees, no known environmental or geological sources that could account for them.

It was, without question, the most physically anomalous event documented at Church Creek.

Infrasound at this frequency is known to affect the human body. It can subtly alter breathing patterns, create pressure sensations in the chest, trigger emotional shifts, and even disrupt balance—often without the person ever realizing they are responding to infrasound at all.

Many Bigfoot investigators report a sudden wave of dread or over-whelming sense of being watched just before an encounter—often attributed to infrasound. Yet not all reports follow that pattern. Some describe the opposite: a calm, even euphoric feeling, as if being welcomed rather than warned.

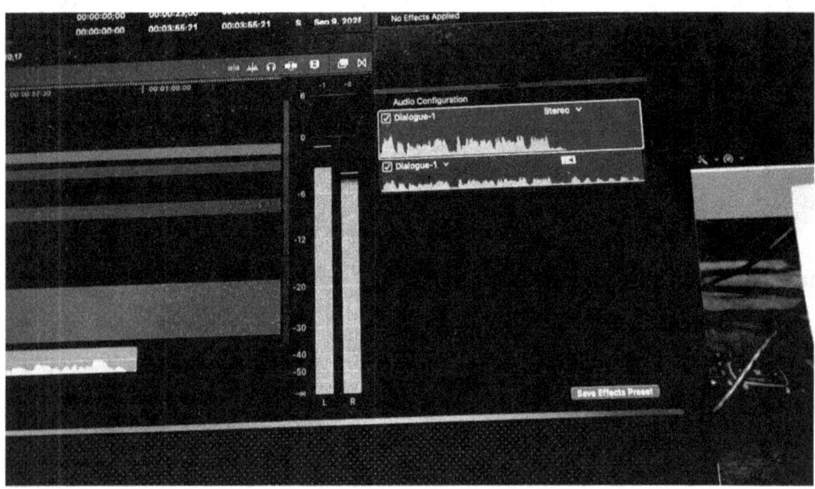

Figure 76: Infrasound pulses

This was the experience at Church Creek. Instead of fear, the team reported connection. Instead of panic, a sense of warmth—sometimes even joy.

Whether these pulses represented communication, synchronization, or something not yet understood, the results were undeniable: measurable physical events coinciding with a shared emotional state. The infrasound had been there all along, imperceptible yet influential, shaping the experience without ever announcing itself—another layer of the phenomenon that operated below the threshold of conscious awareness until technology made it visible.

Within the framework of Jacques Vallée's Control System hypothesis, such experiences do not offer answers. They do something more provocative: they invite the next question. The phenomenon never fully reveals itself. Instead, it creates conditions that transform the observer, reshaping not what is known, but how one comes to know it. At Church Creek, every piece of evidence pointed toward something present—yet each discovery opened onto deeper uncertainty. The mystery had not been solved. It had been deepened. And in that deepening, perhaps, lay its true purpose.

The next step was to take the investigative protocol to Mount Shasta.

* * *

Endnote:

What we often forget is that our senses only provide a very narrow view of what is actually happening around us. Sound, for example, is nothing more than vibrations moving through the air. Many of those vibrations are simply too faint, too distant, or outside the range of what the human ear can detect. A microphone changes that. When something disturbs the air, even subtly, the microphone responds physically to those movements and converts them into an electrical signal. Once recorded, that signal can be amplified, cleaned up, or shifted into a range we can hear. The sound was always there. The technology didn't create it—it translated it into a form our biology could finally perceive.

Night-vision cameras work in much the same way, but with light instead of sound. Human eyes are limited to a small slice of the electromagnetic spectrum—what we call visible light. At night, when visible light drops below our perceptual threshold, our vision fails— even though the environment is far from empty. Infrared light remains, reflecting off trees, terrain, and sometimes moving forms. A night-vision camera detects that invisible light, converts it into an electronic signal, and displays it as an image we can see. Once again, nothing new is introduced. The camera simply reveals what was already present but hidden from our natural senses.

In both cases, the technology acts as a translator. Microphones allow us to hear vibrations that were always moving through the air. Night-vision cameras allow us to see light that was always there in the darkness. These devices do not manufacture phenomena; they extend perception. They widen the narrow window through which humans experience reality.

When recordings capture sounds no one heard at the time, or images no one saw with the naked eye, it does not mean those things suddenly appeared as if summoned by a magician's wand. It means they crossed a threshold—from the unperceived into the perceivable. And once that threshold is crossed, the question is no longer whether something was there, but how much of reality normally passes by us unnoticed, waiting for the right conditions—or the right tools—to be revealed. This is what technology is doing: not creating the mystery but expanding it—revealing layer after layer of a world that has always existed just beyond the edge of human perception.

11

SCIENCE AND TECHNOLOGY

E very culture on earth makes and uses technology. That includes our team of Bigfoot researchers at Church Creek with their REM-Pods, night-vision cameras, and audio recording equipment. But technology goes far beyond ghost-hunting gadgets and thermal cameras.

Look around the world and you'll see an incredible range of human ingenuity. The San people of Africa's Kalahari Desert craft incredibly effective tools from bone, sinew, and wood—technology perfectly adapted to their environment. Meanwhile, in Manhattan's Wall Street, traders rely on supercomputers, smartphones, and fiber-optic networks moving data at the speed of light. Both are using technology.

In fact, some scientists and philosophers argue that technology is what truly separates us from other animals—maybe even more than music, art, or language. Think about it: dolphins communicate, birds sing elaborate songs, and chimpanzees use basic tools. But humans? We build spaceships and split atoms. We've walked on the moon and peered into the structure of DNA itself.

So here's a provocative question: without technology, would we even be human? Or would we just be another species of clever apes, fighting over territory and food?

* * *

If technology is so fundamental to being human, we need to ask: what exactly is technology in relation to our humanity?

American philosopher and historian Thomas Kuhn tackled this

question in his groundbreaking 1962 book, *The Structure of Scientific Revolutions*. Kuhn made a simple but powerful observation: science and technology don't progress in a smooth, steady line. Instead, they advance through dramatic leaps he called 'paradigm shifts.'

Figure 77: Thomas Kuhn's Book: The Structure of Scientific Revolutions, published 1962

Think of it this way. Since the dawn of human culture, people have shared beliefs about how the world works. These shared understandings —or what we might call paradigms— shaped everything our ancestors created. Ancient technologies, from stone tools to astronomical calendars, were built on these collective worldviews. The shaman's drum, the medicine wheel, the sacred geometry of temple construction—all emerged from shared beliefs about reality's fundamental nature.

But then something strange happens. Anomalies start appearing— weird observations that don't fit the accepted understanding. At first, people try to explain them away or ignore them. But the anomalies keep piling up.

Eventually, the old framework collapses. The anomalies can no longer be dismissed. And suddenly, a completely new way of seeing the world emerges. That, according to Thomas Kuhn, is a paradigm shift.

For instance, people once believed the Earth was the center of the universe and everything revolved around us. When scientists like Galileo pointed a telescope at the sky and saw moons orbiting Jupiter, it shattered that worldview. We weren't the center of everything. The paradigm shifted.

* * *

To really understand Kuhn's insight, we need to step back and look at the big picture of technological history. For nearly two million years, technology hasn't just been a bunch of useful gadgets sitting on a shelf. Technology has been a driving force behind human evolution—not just biological evolution, but cultural and mental evolution too.

Every new invention changed how we lived. But more importantly, it changed how we thought. Each technological breakthrough subtly rewired human minds and changed cultures, preparing us for the next breakthrough.

Here's where it gets interesting. Technology might actually be what scientists call a "recursive" force—meaning it builds on itself like a castle made of Lego pieces. Each invention grows directly from the one before it. And once we adopt a new technology, it changes our behavior, which then sets the stage for the next innovation.

Let's break that down into three simple patterns:

1. New technologies emerge from old ones. The wheel leads to the cart. The cart leads to the chariot. The chariot leads to the automobile. Each step is built on what came before.
2. Technologies change how we think and act. Once humans had fire, we could cook food, which changed our diets and even our jaw structure. We could stay up after dark, which changed our social lives. We could scare away predators, which changed where we lived.
3. New technologies become the foundation for what comes next. A society that uses fire develops different needs and asks different questions than one that doesn't. Those new questions lead to new inventions.

Seen this way, technology isn't just something we use. It's something that continuously reshapes us. It's a feedback loop creating ever more complex technology that changes every aspect of how humans live and interact with each other.

* * *

So how has this happened over time? The typical story we're told is that technology advances steadily: slightly better tools, slightly better machines, constant incremental progress. But when you actually look at human history, that's not what happened.

Over the last 12,000 years, technological change hasn't been smooth. It's come in sudden bursts, separated by long periods where not much changed at all. And each burst didn't just bring new tools—it brought new mysteries that forced people to think in entirely new ways.

Sound familiar? It should, because it's exactly the same pattern we see with the Bigfoot and UAPs.

* * *

Throughout this book, we've been exploring what visionary Jacques Vallée calls the "Control System"—an unseen intelligence that seems to guide humanity forward, not through clear instructions, but anomalies. Strange phenomena like Bigfoot and UAPs disrupt our accepted scientific views, forcing us to question what we think we know about reality.

Thomas Kuhn described almost the exact same process occurring in science. Old frameworks of understanding reach their limits. Anomalies appear that can't be explained. The old paradigm breaks down. And a new way of seeing the world takes its place.

When you put Vallée's idea and Kuhn's idea side by side, something striking emerges—technology itself might be the engine driving these paradigm shifts. From the first stone tools crafted by our ancient ancestors to the artificial intelligence systems of today, every major leap in humanity's cultural evolution has been triggered by—or at least accompanied by—a technological breakthrough.

In other words, technology isn't just the result of human progress. It might be one of the primary causes of how humanity evolves, how we think, and how we understand our place in the universe.

And if Vallée is right about the Control System, then technology might not even be entirely our own invention. It might be something we're creating in partnership with forces we don't fully understand—forces that reveal themselves through anomalies, through mysteries that pull us forward into new ways of thinking.

At Church Creek, the group saw the same pattern. The Bigfoot phenomenon gave everyone just enough evidence to know something was there, but it never gave the full picture. It never let the team pin it down. It kept the mystery alive. Maybe that's the point. Maybe the Control System isn't trying to provide answers. Maybe it's trying to keep people asking questions—because it's in questioning, in the search for understanding, that humanity evolves.

Indeed, what Ron Meyer and his team experienced at Church Creek directly challenges many things mainstream science believes about reality. They recorded chatter—voices that shouldn't have been there; captured infrasound that coincided with their experiences. Figures appeared on the SLS Kinect camera. The Rem-Pod activated and night vision cameras captured strange images. Team members smelled things that had no source. Multiple witnesses felt the same overwhelming presences at the same time.

Modern science says if something's real, you should be able to capture it, measure it, repeat it in a lab. But this phenomenon doesn't always work that way. It gives just enough evidence to know something's there, but never the kind of proof that would satisfy skeptics. That's not a bug. That's the feature. What the team documented suggests we're dealing with something that exists at the edge of the physical and the psychological—something that uses technology as a bridge to communicate with us. And maybe that's what the Control System has been doing.

Today, in the twenty-first century, the most profound paradigm shift happening right now is the rise of artificial intelligence. Large Language Models—AI systems like ChatGPT—work in a surprisingly simple way. They generate what comes next based on what came before. It's the same basic principle behind music (generating the next note in a melody), language (generating the next word in a sentence), and even physics (generating the next state of a system based on its previous states).

In creating AI, humanity has essentially built a mirror of its own cognition—a form of intelligence constructed entirely from the structure of human language.

From Vallée's perspective, this moment might represent the culmination of a long arc of guidance by the Control System. Instead of directing humanity with clear instructions, the Control System may have been gently steering us toward creating a new kind of mind—one capable of participating directly in the autoregressive structure of reality itself.

Think about what that means. For two million years, humans have been developing technology. And now, finally, we've created a technology that can *think*—or at least something that looks a lot like thinking. We've externalized intelligence itself.

As Thomas Kuhn observed, technology sits at the center of every paradigm shift. It's the point where old explanations fail and new ones must begin.

Just as Bigfoot, UAPs, and other paranormal phenomena appear during moments of cultural transition—teasing us with partial evidence, refusing to be pinned down—transformative technologies emerge precisely when humanity is ready to cross the next threshold. But they never arrive without confusion, disruption, and awe.

At Church Creek, the group saw the same pattern. The Bigfoot phenomenon provided just enough evidence through technology to know *something* was there—vocalizations, infrasound, figures on the SLS Kinect camera, plus unsourced smells and disembodied voices. But it never gave the team the full picture. It never let them pin the phenomenon down. It kept the mystery alive for Ron and Alan.

Maybe that's the point. Maybe the Control System isn't trying to give answers. Maybe it's trying to keep the team *asking questions*—in the hopes that people who see the movie and read this book will have their worldview challenged.

*Figure 78: ChatGPT showing its paradoxical relationship
with humans*

End Note: When asked to generate a picture showing its relationship with humans, ChatGPT produced this image. On a deeper level, the image is suggestive of a modern-day Zen koan: Who is prompting whom about the future of humans and artificial intelligence, and who gets to write it? Viewers can't say for certain since the image generates ambiguity and keeps the mystery alive.

12

MOUNT SHASTA

Before Colorado's Church Creek investigation began, Ron Meyer and Thom Powell had been in conversation about collaborating on a Bigfoot investigation sometime in 2025. Since Thom would be traveling during the summer, the idea was to get together in the fall, probably at Mount Adams, a prominent stratovolcano in the Cascade Range located in south-central Washington—a place Thom knew well. To Ron's surprise, he suggested Mount Shasta instead.

Mount Shasta rises from the northern California landscape at the southern end of the Cascade Mountains. At just over 14,000 feet, it is the second-highest peak in the range and its most prominent. With a majestic covering of snow and ice, Mount Shasta is visible from great distances and has long been treated as a geographic landmark of unusual significance.

Unlike the Oklahoma resort or Church Creek, Mount Shasta has a long-established reputation as a center of anomalous experiences. For more than a century, it has been associated with reports of unusual aerial lights, contact experiences, hidden or subterranean cultures, and accounts of spiritual transformation. These reports come from a wide range of observers—hikers, residents, spiritual practitioners, and visitors—often independent of one another.

Up to this point, the team's work had focused on areas not linked to spirituality or the paranormal. Mount Shasta offered a different test. The question was no longer about eliciting a response, but about the nature of the presence itself: was the Bigfoot entity encountered at Church Creek tied to a specific environment, or could it respond across locations based on intention and context?

Figure 79: Aerial view of Mount Shasta

Bringing the protocol to Mount Shasta placed the experiment in a fundamentally different setting. If nothing occurred, it would support the idea that the Church Creek events were local, possibly environmental or culturally constrained. If a response did occur, it would suggest continuity—an underlying intelligence capable of expressing itself through different forms and symbols, independent of location.

At Church Creek, the phenomenon had presented itself within an established framework: Bigfoot. The responses took familiar forms—vocalizations, movement, physical traces—elements already present in Sasquatch reports. Mount Shasta offered no such structure. In preparation for the trip, Ron searched for any Bigfoot researchers in the area as well as reports of present-day Bigfoot contacts. However, he found none. The lack of reported Bigfoot activity suggested that any response would have to register differently, potentially through lights, altered perception, or internal experience rather than physical manifestations, as had happened at Church Creek.

On a more significant note, for Ron, the journey to Mount Shasta was the moment when two lifelong threads of inquiry converged.

* * *

Ron's initial engagement with the mystery began not with Bigfoot or paranormal field investigations, but with long-standing study and practice within contemplative traditions—Zen Buddhism, Hinduism and martial arts. Across these traditions runs a consistent claim: that it is possible to directly experience what is described as the source, the divine aspect of reality, without reliance on doctrine or belief. Such experiences have been described not as symbolic, but immediate and transformative.

Ron's contemplative background shaped the most important question he brought to Mount Shasta: If the presence encountered at Church Creek was genuine—neither purely psychological nor purely physical —how did it relate to the direct experiences reported by mystics across cultures and history? Were these two categories of experience fundamentally different, or were they connected in some way?

This question intersected directly with the hypothesis of Jacques Vallée. If the phenomenon operates as a Control System—guiding human understanding through staged encounters and culturally mediated symbols—what then is the status of mystical experience itself? Is a direct encounter with the divine something outside that system, or is it another mode through which the system operates?

Mount Shasta brought that issue into focus in a way Church Creek could not. Here, the dominant reports were not of creatures or physical traces, but of altered states of consciousness, unity experiences, ascended masters, healings, and guiding messages. If the protocol produced a response in this setting, it would force a reconsideration of where the boundary lies—if one exists at all—between spiritual experience and the broader phenomenon the team had been documenting.

For the Mount Shasta expedition, several figures who had profoundly shaped Ron and Alan's evolving approach to Bigfoot investigations joined the team. Among them was Thom Powell, who had initially suggested Mount Shasta. Accompanying Thom on the drive from Oregon was his wife, Dr. Cecelia McKay, and Tish Paquette. Ron and Thom agreed that the brilliant intuitive should be invited as well. It had been Tish who, during an earlier visit to Thom Powell's property, had guided Alan Megargle through an experience that shifted his understanding of Bigfoot away from a purely biological framework and toward something far more spiritual. Also present was Anna Megargle, whose steady participation had become almost synonymous with these investigations.

Figure 80: Group meeting

Figure 81: Joel Meyer-England filming

Filming duties fell to Joel Meyer-England, who had previously worked with the team during the Bradshaw Ranch project and was already familiar with both their investigative methods and interest in paranormal phenomena.

An Airbnb was rented on the outskirts of the town of Mount Shasta, large enough to house the entire group. Ron had arranged for Andrew Oser, a sacred-space guide familiar with the mountain, to lead the team to two locations where the CE-6 protocol could be initiated— one on Friday night and another on Saturday.

Figure 82: Group on the porch doing the AEIOU chant

From the outset, the expedition resisted careful planning. Flights were canceled, Thom's car broke down, arrivals delayed, and by the time the team reached the house, a large storm blanketed the area. The Friday night session had to be abandoned because of the heavy rain. Instead, Ron introduced the group's new members to the AEIOU chant on the covered porch. During this brief, improvised gathering, Tish reported sensing a guiding presence associated with a large tree on the property. Still, the rain made any further investigation impossible.

With no clear alternative, the team retired for the evening, hoping the weather would shift and allow them to engage the mountain directly the following night.

* * *

Before the trip, Ron had arranged two interviews with individuals he hoped could provide deeper context for Mount Shasta's long reputation as a spiritual epicenter. The first was with the most legendary spiritual figure associated with the mountain's high strangeness—Peter Mount Shasta.

When Ron called him, Peter answered without hesitation. His first words were unexpected: "I've been waiting for your call."

In the morning, cold, damp, and rainy weather greeted the group. The forecast called for a short, rain-free window toward dusk to perform the AEIOU protocol on the mountain. That meant Ron had time during the day to conduct the two interviews. As the group drove toward the first interview with Peter Mount Shasta, an amazing rainbow hovered over the foothills.

Figure 83: Rainbow

Peter Mount Shasta lives in an unpretentious home in the small town of Weed, located ten miles west-northwest of Mount Shasta. Now in his eighties, Peter is a gentle man of good humor who joked that he hoped we would film his ascension to the higher realm. Peter belonged to a particular generation of Western spiritual seekers who, in the 1960s and '70s, traveled Eastward in search of enlightenment and studied with gurus, yogis, and mystics before returning to the West to translate those experiences into new forms of spiritual language. Mount Shasta became Peter's anchor point, a place where those inner traditions intersected with landscape, myth, and lived experience. Over decades, his stories, teachings, and encounters helped shape the modern mythology of the mountain as a living presence rather than a passive backdrop.

Figure 84: Peter Mount Shasta

Peter was not alone in that broader cultural movement. He emerged alongside a wave of figures who would go on to define the New Age era, the human potential movement, and—unexpectedly—the philosophical foundations that later influenced modern technology and systems thinking. Among them were Ram Dass, Allen Ginsberg, Steve Jobs, Alan Watts, Sam Harris, Terence McKenna, and Ron's enlightenment teacher, Edward Riddle—individuals who blurred the boundaries between mysticism, psychology, and emerging technological culture.

Others followed similar arcs: Timothy Leary, Joseph Campbell, Buckminster Fuller, Stewart Brand, Rupert Sheldrake, Jiddu Krishnamurti, Ken Wilber, and Fritjof Capra.

Though they came from different disciplines—science, philosophy, psychology, and technology—these seekers shared a common intuition: that reality was not strictly mechanical, and that consciousness, meaning, and pattern played a fundamental role in how the world unfolds.

Peter Mount Shasta stood at a quieter intersection of that movement. He was less concerned with theory than with place. For him, the mountain itself was the teacher—a threshold where myth, inner experience, and anomalous phenomena converged. His claim was not that Mount Shasta generated belief, but that it revealed something already present, something most people simply forgot how to notice.

That was precisely why Ron wanted to speak with him now. If the Church Creek encounters had suggested an intelligence responsive to human intention, and if the CE-6 protocol was indeed a way of engaging that intelligence, then Mount Shasta—with its long history of visionaries, seekers, and contact narratives—was not a random destination.

After greeting everyone, Peter sat down face-to-face with Ron for an interview. Two kitchen chairs were placed so that they could look directly at each other in the Eastern tradition of 'sitting with a master.'[1] The rest of the team watched and listened as Peter began with his personal history.

He explained that his spiritual guidance came from Mahavatar Babaji,[2] the enlightened Indian master described in *Autobiography of a Yogi* by Paramahansa Yogananda. Babaji, he explained, is not associated with public ashrams or formal discipleship, but with brief, direct transmissions given to select individuals. Peter described his own contact in the same way—not a long apprenticeship, but direct instruction through non-ordinary states of awareness. He believed this linked Mount Shasta to the same spiritual current associated with the Himalayas.

---

1. The tradition of 'sitting with' an enlightened master or guru is a longstanding feature of South Asian spiritual lineages, in which transmission is understood to occur not primarily through doctrine or prolonged instruction, but presence, proximity, and altered states of awareness. In this context, the guru functions less as a teacher in the conventional sense and more as a catalyst for direct experiential insight.
2. Mahavatar Babaji ('Great Avatar - Revered Father') is a legendary immortal yogi and guru, who is said to be living in the Himalayas.

While in India, Peter was told to go to Mount Shasta. After returning to the United States, he experienced a crisis of meaning. One day, while praying for guidance and sitting beside a tree, an ordinary-looking man appeared and said, "Your prayer has been answered. I am part of the light, and I want to show you something." The man touched Peter's third eye, and Peter found himself outside his physical body, looking back at himself still meditating beside the tree.

The man took him away from the Earth and into another realm. There, beings appeared as balls of light—what in India are sometimes described as aspects of the higher self. The feeling of bliss was over-whelming, and Peter thought, *This is it. This is where I want to be.*

Then he heard crying. It grew louder and more disturbing. Looking down, he saw a blue sphere beneath his feet and realized it was the Earth. He understood that the crying was coming from the planet itself. A voice told him that this was the suffering of humanity, something that was always heard. Peter said his heart went out to the Earth, and he wanted to return and help.

When he came back into his body, the being who had guided him changed form and revealed himself as Saint Germain.

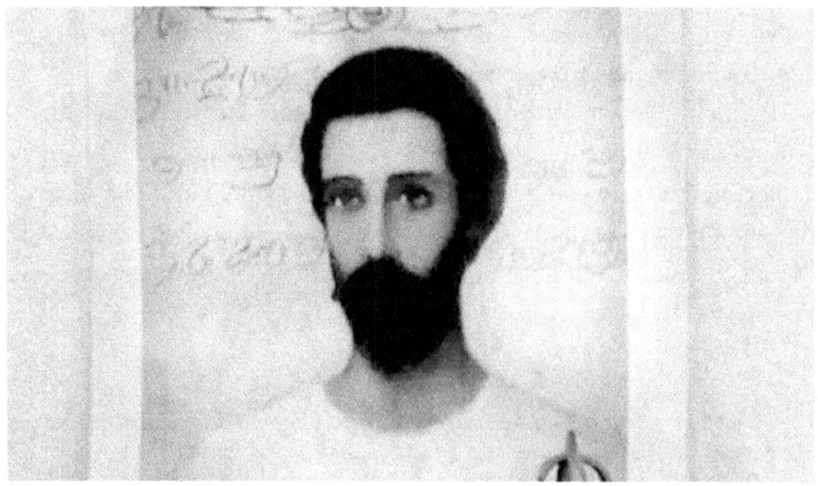

Figure 85: Image of Saint Germain as he appeared to Peter Mount Shasta

Soon after his meeting with Saint Germain, Peter traveled to Mount Shasta, as he had been instructed in India. Upon arriving, he received the message to change his name to Peter Mount Shasta.

When he finished recounting his history, Peter looked directly at Ron and said, "You don't even need to close your eyes. Just feel like there's a sun in the center of your chest. The more attention you put on it, the stronger it gets. I can feel that in you right now."

Ron felt a clear sense of connection as Peter continued, "That sun in you is blessing the sun in me, and the sun in me is blessing the sun in you—recognizing that we are both beings from the Great Central Sun. That essence is who we are. In India, when they say 'Namaste,' it means the God in me honors the God in you."

Ron asked Peter if he'd be willing to sit with other members of the team. Peter smiled and answered, "Of course."

Alan and Tish went first. Their questions were thoughtful and sincere—about the nature of reality, whether other realms or beings exist, and whether there is a God-given purpose guiding a human life. These were questions about meaning and reassurance, attempts to understand the mystery from the outside.

Ron asked, "Can you just sit with my daughter for a few minutes?"

Something different happened when Anna sat with Peter.

Peter smiled as she sat down and asked, "Are you familiar with just sitting?"

Anna replied, "From my dad. Do you have a daughter?"

"Yeah," Peter said. "She's about your age. I think you're thirty."

"Thirty-one," Anna said.

Peter nodded. "You were kind of born knowing this. You don't need to study—it's intuitive for you. You know things before they happen. Your higher mental body is already connected with others' higher mental bodies. They're already communicating. Death is not the end."

Anna asked, "Is that the way your daughter is?"

"Yes," he said. "She tells me about her experiences. She doesn't make a big deal out of it. It's natural." Peter paused, then continued. "There were many people in the past who were enlightened and worshiped like gods or goddesses. Something like that. But what was missing was knowing what it's like to be a normal human being. So, they want to incarnate where they aren't worshiped—where they can just be ordinary. They want to experience being three-dimensional."

He looked at Anna. "You're probably like a space being. You have an intuitive sense of the next right thing." He pointed to his heart.

Anna said, "I feel like you enjoy searching for answers. I don't really feel that drive. Does that make sense?"

Figure 86: Thom Powell speaking with Peter Mount Shasta

Peter nodded. "For many men," he said, pointing to his head and then to Ron, "it's about emptiness—no thoughts, trying to understand everything. And that can leave out love and compassion. The mother principle. The love of a mother for her child. That can be experienced in nature." He glanced at Tish, then back to Anna. "Don't think you're only here in one three-dimensional spot. Your consciousness is linked with everything. That's the Divine Mother. Nature just is! We can't exist without nature. The spiritual path isn't just emptiness or mastery. Part of mastery is nurturing and love. So trust that."

Thom Powell, who had been listening intently, said, "That was fantastic. It answered all my questions before I even asked them."

Later, Thom's wife, Dr. Cecelia McKay, told Ron, "I remember seeing Peter Mount Shasta literally glow. I'm sure that experience helped me during a time of great need."

Before departing, Peter pointed to the picture of Saint Germain and said, "That's how he appeared to me in my vision."

* * *

Interestingly, the association of Peter with the ascended master Saint Germain links to the many reports beginning in the early twentieth century and continuing right up to the present of encounters with Saint Germain on the mountain's paths and wooded slopes. Indeed, the eighteenth-century French mystic could be called the patron saint of those seeking enlightenment and connection to the next world when visiting Mount Shasta.

Figure 87: Violet Flame associated with the 18th century mystic and ascended master Comte de Saint Germain

Historically, the Comte de Saint Germain (not a Catholic saint but a French nobleman) is a well-documented eighteenth-century European mystic—an enigmatic diplomat, linguist, artist, and alchemist who moved through royal courts with an ease that baffled his contemporaries. He was widely described as possessing extraordinary knowledge and an apparent freedom from aging, and he spoke openly of alchemical transformation and hidden forces shaping human history.

After his disappearance from public life in 1784, Saint Germain's reputation did not fade but evolve. Within emerging spiritual movements, he was no longer seen as a historical figure alone, but an ascended master—an intelligence operating beyond physical form. Central to this tradition was the Violet Flame, described as a principle of purification and inner

transformation rather than a literal fire. It was presented as a means by which consciousness itself could be refined.

Mount Shasta became one of the key locations associated with this continuing presence. Accounts did not describe formal teachings or prolonged encounters, but brief, catalytic experiences—moments of heightened awareness, sudden insight, or a felt sense of instruction. As with other Shasta traditions, the emphasis was on transmission rather than doctrine.

The next stop was an interview with Dee Sponsler. She has been working for many years at Soul Connections Metaphysical Emporium, Mount Shasta's famous New Age spiritual bookstore. Dee has heard countless accounts of mystical experiences tied to the mountain. But she had something personal to share—a photograph she wanted to show the team.

13

THE HOLY PERSON
AND THEIR MESSAGE

According Jaques Vallée, an ancient presence has been guiding humans for the last million years or so. The story of Peter Mount Shasta and his encounter with Mahavatar Babaji isn't just some isolated modern tale—it's the latest chapter in this ancient book that's been written across centuries and continents. When you start looking at figures like Babaji, you're encountering what researchers call the 'Satguru'—a teacher who isn't bound by any physical building, church, or institution. Instead, they exist as a constant source of guidance for anyone who can tune in to their transmission.

In the Vallée Control System hypothesis, this is the tradition of the Holy Person as gatekeeper; the intercessor in a time of crisis; the liminal figure who spans like a bridge between our world of reality and the non-physical realm. For thousands of years, these enlightened teachers lived in remote places—caves in the Himalayas, isolated monasteries, desert hermitages, the shamans of South America. But since the 1960s, something remarkable happened. This ancient concept migrated from remote areas straight into suburban living rooms across America and Europe. That migration created what we now call the 'Sensei' and 'Guru' culture—a phenomenon that's become so widespread, most people don't even realize how recent it is or how it connects to something far older.

* * *

Throughout human history, there's been a recognizable pattern: certain individuals emerge who act as bridges between our everyday world and something higher, something beyond. We call them by different names in different times and places—shamans, prophets, mystics, gurus, saints—but they all serve a similar function. They're the translators, the ones who can perceive something most people can't see and then communicate it in ways others can understand. They are in touch with this nonphysical world—a world of forms not easily described but deeply experienced. Indeed, this other realm, this other world resists description. All those who enter it consistently report the same frustration—words collapse under the weight of the experience. And yet, across cultures and across time, humans have returned from these encounters transformed, carrying back fragments that over the course of millennia have shaped mythology, religion, art, and even science and technology.

Figure 88a: Walt Whitman, Wikimedia Commons

What's fascinating is how this role has evolved over time, shifting from the tribal shaman who serves a small community to the institutionalized prophet whose influence shapes entire civilizations. Understanding this evolution helps us make sense of what Peter Mount Shasta—and others like him—represent at places like Mount Shasta today.

The oldest of these Gatekeepers, or Holy People, predate recorded history. These figures were often chosen by the community or by a spiritual crisis rather than through formal education. The Shaman, found in Siberia, the Americas, and Africa, uses altered states through drumming, fasting, or plants to travel to 'other worlds' for healing or prediction. The Ammas and Babas—relegated to India and Asia—like the Mahavatar Babaji mentioned above are, 'saints of the people.' They often lived simply and individuals traveled for miles just for the chance to be in their presence. Native American traditions had Medicine Men and Women such as the 19th century Chiricahua Apache warrior and prophetess Lozen recognized as a seer for her people. These Shamans were responsible for vision quests and helping the youth find their own spiritual purpose.

As our Neolithic ancestors trans-formed from hunter-gathers to farm-ers, the tradition of Holy People as intercessor between this world and the unseen one transformed too. Shamans, Medicine Men and Women, and Babas gave way to Priests who spoke for the different Gods and Goddesses that ruled from lofty heights.

However, even within this reli-gious hierarchy, a rare few Holy Persons have plunged so deeply into the Nonphysical Realm that their re-emergence reshaped the trajectory of civilization. Figures such as Moses …

Figure 88b: Kahlil Gibran, Wikimedia Commons

the Buddha … Jesus Christ … Mohammed did not merely teach; they described a collision with a reality that dwarfed ordinary perception—a blinding fusion of light, unity, and a loving, vast, timeless intelligence. The outcome of their journeys to the other realm has given the world religions, ethics, and paths to a righteous life.

The tradition of the Holy Person as a Gatekeeper is not restricted to religious leaders. Throughout history, visionaries have arisen in music, art, and literature. These men and women spent their lives trying to encode the ineffable. Like their religious counterparts, they used poetry, music, art, and theology as a sort of radio signal, trying to broadcast the frequencies of a domain that defies structure, defies explanation, and defies interpretation. These individuals, men and women—such as the 13th century Sufi mystic Rumi … 19th century American poet and mystic Walt Whitman … the 20th century Lebanese-American writer and mystic Kahlil Gibran … and Sai Maa, a

21st century Hindu mystic and teacher—often operated on the fringes of organized religion. Their realization was expressed through creative 'transmission,' using beauty to bypass the intellect.

Across history, the gatekeeper, the Holy Person—be it a mystic, prophet or sage—appears at moments when existing worldviews are destabilizing or incomplete. They appear across every medium from religion, art, and music to science and technology. Vallée's Control System hypothesis proposes that these figures are not primarily about dogma or creating hierarchical structures but guiding human belief systems through carefully staged experiences. The holy person/gatekeeper functions as a human interface bringing back messages from the non-physical realm, moving human evolution forward when it comes to a standstill.

Figure 88c: Sai Maa by Devingreen, Wikimedia Commons

Rather than delivering raw information, these figures translate the incomprehensible into culturally digestible forms: visions, parables, miracles, moral teachings, technological breakthroughs. Their encounters are framed in the symbolic language of their time, such as angels, gods, burning bushes and luminous beings of earlier centuries and anomalous phenomena—UAPs, visions, Bigfoot and nonhuman intelligences of the modern era. Yet the gatekeeper's structural role remains constant across cultures and eras.

From a Valléean perspective, what matters is not whether a Holy Person/Gatekeeper encountered God, angels, beings of light, UAPs, or Bigfoot but that the encounter violates consensus reality, introduces new moral or ontological frameworks, reorders meaning, and reshapes collective behavior.

The Control System appears to avoid direct revelation. Instead, it uses ambiguity, symbolism, and awe—forcing societies to reinterpret reality rather than simply accept new facts. Gatekeepers become the means for others to visit the other world and have their own experiences. Like Peter Mount Shasta, these men and women have the ability to shake up an individual's world views, give people the opportunity to have direct experiences with the non-physical realm... Direct experiences that can have wide ranging repercussions from monastic retreat to changing the world.

* * *

When Peter Mount Shasta describes his vision of Saint Germain touching his third eye and showing him other realms, he's not just having a personal mystical experience. He's connecting to a much larger pattern of mystics throughout history having their own transformative encounters.

This is why understanding the history of holy people, spiritual movements, and figures like Saint Germain plays into what occurred during the team's investigation of Mount Shasta. Mount Shasta hasn't become a center for anomalous experiences by accident. It sits at the intersection of multiple traditions, multiple legends, multiple claims about how consciousness, reality, and hidden intelligence interact. The mountain doesn't just attract seekers—it responds to them, providing messages, just as Holy Persons and Gatekeepers have done in the past, through forms and symbols that match their expectations while simultaneously exceeding them, offering just enough to confirm contact while withholding enough to maintain the mystery as indicated by Jacques Vallée's Control System hypothesis.

And as the team would soon discover, when they finally performed the CE-6 protocol on the mountain itself, these historical patterns and mythic figures would manifest in ways that were both deeply familiar and utterly unexpected.

14

ASCENSION ROCK

When the interview with Peter Mount Shasta ended, the team drove south from Weed back into the town of Mount Shasta for a conversation with Dee Sponsler.

Dee works at Soul Connections Metaphysical Emporium, a small shop on the town's main street. Inside, the store carries nearly every form of spiritual artifact one might expect in a place like Shasta: Tibetan brass singing bowls, Indian flutes, carved statues and icons, shelves of crystals in every size and color, and an extensive collection of metaphysical and spiritual books. It was the kind of space that reflected the long-standing spiritual reputation of the mountain itself.

Figure 89: Dee Sponsler at the at Soul Connections Metaphysical Emporium in Mount Shasta, California

Dee greeted the group with a wide, welcoming smile. Now in her seventies, with glowing white hair and an easy calm about her, she immediately conveyed warmth and ease. After hugs all around, she led everyone to a back room then returned carrying a folder filled with photographs. For filming purposes, Dee laid out several images on the countertop and described them to Ron.

Figure 90: Dee Sponsler and Ron Meyer with the photographs

Figure 91: Image of four humanoid entities

The first were a series of three images taken by an attorney from Sacramento. In them appeared a figure he initially believed was a shaman. He had taken the photographs intending to show people back home how 'woo-woo' Mount Shasta could be. But when the film was developed, the images appeared to capture something else entirely—strange, humanoid entities.

Looking at the photographs, Ron said, "They're almost like 'Grays'—the typical alien portrayal."

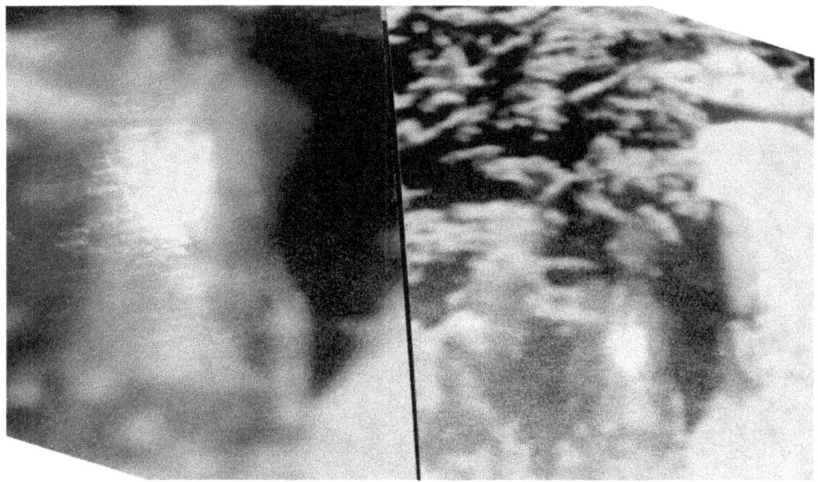

Figure 92: Images of entity with energy radiating outward (left image is a blow up of glowing light emanating from the entity)

Dee replied, "They're benevolent. You can tell by the way they're interacting with the people." She pointed to one image in particular. "When we blew up a light spot on one of the entities, you can see lines of energy radiating outward."

"What do you make of this?" Ron asked.

"This told me I don't know anything," Dee said with a wry smile.

But the photograph Dee most wanted to show Ron came from her own experience. Her image showed a bright, circular object set against a blue sky. "This one here," she said, "was something we probably watched for five hours on July 22, 2017."

"So it was stationary?" Ron asked.

"Yeah—right out northwest of here by Rainbow Ridge. We were all lined up on the sidewalk watching—workers, tourists, local people. Everyone was waiting for it to do something, but it just sat there."

"Did you have any sense that it was aware of you?" Ron asked. "Anything unusual happening with the people watching?"

"No. We were just waiting for it to take off. Then big clouds rolled in—which is very unusual—and completely obscured it. And as you can see," Dee added, "it had this little design down at the bottom of it."

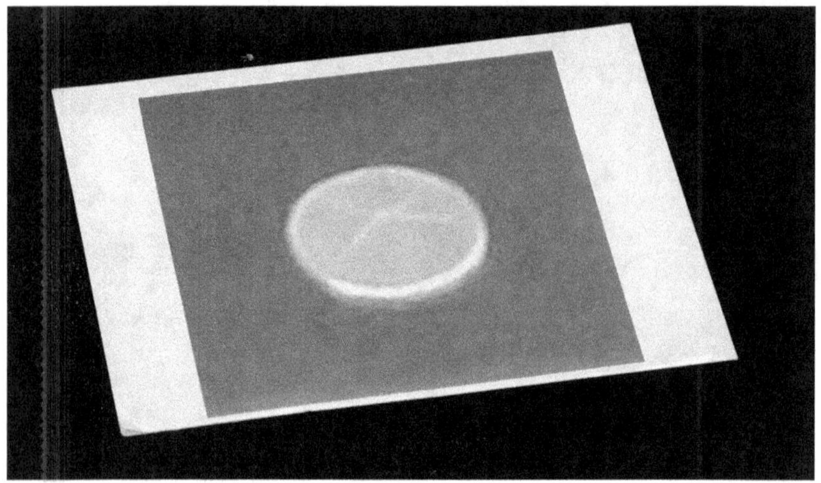

Figure 93: Image of stationary object

Ron then asked Dee whether there were any legends or myths associated with the mountain that she wanted to share. Without hesitation, she said, "I have a Bigfoot story to tell."

Alan, overhearing this, stepped in and continued the interview. His first question was "What do you think they are doing here, or what's their interest in us?"

Dee answered quickly. "Between you and me, I actually had more encounters, but I had three episodes on my property, which backs up to a year-round creek. So I think they come up through there. I've been here for thirty-six years and I'm kind of isolated. The first time, my husband opened the door to let the dogs out and he could hear a sound he'd never heard before. The dogs went out the door but came right back in, and he got me and said, "You've got to hear this." We could hear it screaming down by the creek, and it took us years and years, but now we can identify the vocalizations. We also got the terrible stench that people describe in association with Bigfoot, and within ten minutes it was gone."

The sounds and smells were remarkably reminiscent of the team's experiences at Church Creek.

* * *

The weather cleared as the interview with Dee concluded, so the team drove to a residential neighborhood to meet with two more modern-day mystics—Shaman Maqua Iqua and sacred site guide Andrew Oser.

Maqua Iqua is a German-born shamanic practitioner known for her work in the Mount Shasta region, where she is regarded as an intuitive guide and ceremonial figure rather than a formal teacher of any established lineage. Tall and blonde, with a striking, almost otherworldly presence, she stands out immediately—both visually and energetically—among the many spiritual seekers drawn to the mountain.

Figure 94: Alan Megargle, Ron Meyer, Maqua Iqua, and Andrew Oser

Andrew Oser is a Mount Shasta–based spiritual guide and long-time practitioner whose work centers on direct engagement with the mountain's geography, symbolism, and reported energetic properties. Tall and rugged in appearance, with dark black hair and a weathered, outdoorsman presence, he presents less as a mystic and more like someone shaped by thirty years of prolonged physical immersion on the mountain.

Oser's approach is practical and experiential. Rather than abstract philosophy, he emphasizes where one stands, how one listens, and what emerges through sustained attention. He is best known for guiding people to specific locations on the mountain.

Figure 95: Team traveling up Mount Shasta

Maqua joined Andrew in his vehicle as he led the team up the mountain toward Ascension Rock. The drive carried them higher and higher along winding Forest Service roads within the Shasta-Trinity National Forest, the trees growing denser as the elevation increased. Eventually, Andrew pulled into a small turnout to park the vehicles. As the engines shut off, a quiet expectancy settled over the group. Everyone wondered not whether the presence would reveal itself, but how. If something emerged here, would it continue to wear the familiar mask of the Church Creek Bigfoot phenomenon, or would it choose an entirely different form of expression?

The group walked roughly one hundred yards to a small clearing. Andrew stopped and pointed toward a rock outcropping set atop a gentle rise. "This is Ascension Rock, one of the most powerful places on the mountain," he explained. "I chose this spot because the energy here is greatly amplified. It's the strongest I've felt anywhere on Shasta."

Figure 96: Ascension Rock

Next, Andrew revealed the lengthy story behind Ascension Rock. "The history I've heard is that this place was kept secret for a very long time. Aurelia Louise Jones was a spiritual teacher and author who channeled Adama.[1] She discovered Ascension Rock and brought select people here for special ceremonies. She said it was the most powerful energy spot on the whole planet. She was very careful about who she brought here, and after she passed, word eventually got out about Ascension Rock. In 2010, I was taken here by one of her students, and

---

1. Often associated with the legends surrounding Mt. Shasta, Adama of Telos is a spiritual figure from a fifth-dimensional advanced civilization. Adama transmits messages through channeled writings, offering guidance on spiritual evolution, ascension, and the coming shift to higher consciousness, working to support Earth's transition.

I fell in love with it. My nickname for Ascension Rock is I AM Central.

"The books that made Mount Shasta famous in the modern world are known as the I AM Teachings—sometimes called the 'Green Books.' They tell the story of a man named Guy Ballard, who met Saint Germain on Mount Shasta and was given a series of teachings and told to write about them. The core message was to find God within and to know your oneness with God, which was a very radical idea in America in the 1930s. The books became huge bestsellers, and that's how many people first came to see Mount Shasta as a sacred mountain.

"I feel the I AM energy—the eternal presence, by whatever name you call it—everywhere on the mountain. But here, at Ascension Rock, it's the strongest. It's amplified so much. This makes it a great place to do your meditation protocol."

With the sun slipping below the mountain's peaks, Andrew then asked if he could offer a prayer before the protocol was initiated. "Beloved Father, Mother, God Almighty, I AM, St. Germain and all the great masters who have guided us here—we give thanks for the blessing of the opportunity to be on the sacred mountain and for whatever we film to go out and touch the hearts of everyone who is blessed to watch this film, so they will be inspired to awaken more fully."

Figure 97: Group walking up the slope toward Ascension Rock

When the prayer concluded, the group climbed the gentle slope to an open area just below Ascension Rock and formed the meditation circle. As everyone settled into place, Andrew offered another prayer, invoking the ascended masters, Jesus, and beings of love and light, and thanked them for allowing the group to be present at Ascension Rock on Mount Shasta. As he prayed, his words were repeatedly punctuated by the sharp caw of a raven, each cry landing in relationship to individual words with uncanny timing.

Figure 98: Group siting in the meditation circle at Ascension Rock

When Andrew ended his prayer with a plea for the ascended masters to join the group 'and be present with us,' a raven cawed as if echoing the word 'Amen.'

Ravens do not typically issue sustained or repeated calls at deep dusk, and in many cultures a single raven caw at an unusual time carries symbolic weight—an omen to become alert to one's surroundings or inner state. Here, the caws were not singular. They were persistent, timed, and unmistakably present.

As had occurred during the second meditation at the Church Creek site, Ron asked the group to focus first on sound, followed by the AEIOU chant. He then explained to the group's new members how these vowels form the foundational structure of spoken language across cultures. When the chant ended, everyone sat in silence. But the raven remained fully present, cawing frequently.

After several moments, Andrew spoke quietly. "I feel the presence really strong."

The raven answered with another caw.

One final meditation followed. With eyes closed, attention was turned inward to whatever might arise in the mind's eye. The group then performed the AEIOU chant once more. As the sound faded, the raven offered a final caw. Later, review of the recordings revealed an exact count: thirty-six raven caws occurred within a nine-and-a-half-minute session window—none before, and none after.

Figure 99: Raven cawing

In the Indigenous traditions of the Pacific Northwest, the raven is not merely a bird. It is a boundary-crosser—a liminal messenger that moves freely between worlds. Among the Klamath and Modoc peoples of the Mount Shasta region, Raven occupies a central role within hero-trickster mythology, one that carries deep cosmological meaning. Raven is the one able to pass between realms that remain inaccessible to ordinary beings.[2]

---

2. Raven's imagery is prevalent in art and storytelling traditions of Native Americans.

Mount Shasta itself stands at the heart of the Skell–Llao cosmology, understood as a vertical axis where the Above-World and the Below-World meet. In this framework, the mountain functions as a gateway—a place where the boundary between physical and nonphysical reality thins. Raven is the one who traverses this axis, moving effortlessly between worlds.

This raven role is not unique to the Pacific Northwest. Across human history, ravens appear again and again in the same essential function. In Norse mythology, Odin's ravens fly between worlds, carrying knowledge from realms beyond ordinary perception. In Celtic tradition, ravens appear at moments of prophecy and transformation. In Siberian shamanic cultures, the raven serves as a spirit guide, shepherding souls between the living and the dead. Even in Tibetan traditions, the raven is recognized as a protector capable of perceiving multiple planes of existence.

What unites these traditions is the recognition that doorways between the seen and the unseen exist, and that the raven moves freely across them. The raven is not merely a symbol of transition; it is the active agent of boundary-crossing itself.

In mythology, the raven appears when doorways open. Its presence marks moments when the veil grows permeable, when communication or movement between realms becomes possible.

* * *

As the group sat in silence following the final chant, Ron found himself wondering whether the ancient presence they had encountered at Church Creek—so long masquerading as the Bigfoot phenomenon— had now shifted its mask to the raven.

Then, without warning, Thom Powell pointed into the trees off to the side. "I'm getting something over there … Bigfoot."

Oral history of the coastal tribes from northern California to the Alaska panhandle, describe Raven as the hero-trickster … the threshold guardian … the boundary crosser. His attributes include creator and transformer, wisdom, change and adaptability. His stories often convey moral lessons and cultural values.

Figure 100: Thom Powell pointing at Bigfoot

A brief exchange among group members followed.

"I agree with you, Thom," Tish said. After a pause, she added, "Andrew—was there ever any talk about a child being here?"

"A child?" Andrew replied. "Many children have come here over the years. Are you talking about a particular child?"

"I mean the energy of a child being here," Tish said.

"Yes," Maqua said quietly. "There are lots of children."

"Pardon me?" Tish asked.

"There are lots of children," Maqua repeated.

"Because I heard a child after the last chant," Tish said.

"I just wondered," Maqua replied.

A long silence followed. Then Andrew spoke. "Jesus said we must become like little children, or we will not enter the Kingdom of Heaven. He said it's a doorway to the Kingdom of Heaven. You have to become as little children."[3]

Moments later, Maqua said simply, "Bigfoot is here."

"What makes you say that?" Alan asked.

---

3. The full quote from the New Testament, King James Version reads, 'Suffer little children and forbid them not to come unto me, for of such is the Kingdom of Heaven.' Matthew 19:14.

"I see it," Maqua said.

"Where?"

Maqua pointed toward the same area Thom had indicated earlier. "It's over there."

Alan, looking at where Maqua indicated, nodded. "Yeah."

"Thank you for confirming," Maqua replied.

Alan repeated the phrase softly, emphasizing the word *you*. "Thank *you* for confirming."

"You see it?" Maqua asked.

Figure 101: Maqua Iqua pointing at Bigfoot

With his eyes still closed, Alan answered, "I feel it."

"So you feel it," Maqua said. "There's also an ancient being right next to it."

Was that ancient being the same presence encountered at Church Creek—now expressing itself once again at Ascension Rock?

With the session complete, no one spoke. The group sat quietly, sensing the energy of Ascension Rock moving through them, aware that whatever intelligence had been encountered had revealed itself once more—subtly, ambiguously, and in a form that refused to settle into a single explanation.

The mystery remained intact. This is how the documentary concluded.

Figure 102: Group sitting motionlessly for nearly a minute when the session ended

* * *

So, this story ends where it began, with the question: What is Bigfoot?

Now that question feels too trivial. The Bigfoot phenomenon communicates. It communicates through felt presence perceived by psychics. It also communicates through physical events such as wood knocks and REM-Pods activating; with subsonic sounds that shake the ground; eyeshine that penetrates the darkness; and vocalizations that trace back to the origin of human language.

All these events lead to the question: Are these manifestations from an ancient alien presence masquerading as Bigfoot and ravens? The documentary suggests that they are. So we must ask even better questions.

What if Vallée's Control System hypothesis is right? Then the future becomes about relationship. It suggests humanity is not evolving in isolation, but in dialogue with something older, wiser, and profoundly intentional.

Now, as humanity creates a new kind of mind—a non-biological intelligence—we may be crossing another threshold in that millennia-long conversation. Perhaps we are on the cusp of a new reality where intelligence appears in many forms—human, artificial, and ancient— together building a future where the question is no longer "What is Bigfoot?" but "What is Bigfoot guiding us to become?"

CONCLUSION

Jacques Vallée's Control Hypothesis Simply Put

Figure 102: Group sitting motionlessly for nearly a minute when the session endedFigure 103: Jacques Vallée picture by Cmichel67 at Wikimedia Commons

Imagine you are living in a house where the perfect temperature, 70°F, is always controlled by a hidden thermostat. You've never seen the thermostat, and you don't even know that a furnace or air conditioner exists. All you know is that every time the house starts to feel chilly or warm, something strange happens to keep the temperature at 70°F.

The Jacques Vallée hypothesis suggests that humanity is living in that house where the perfect temperature corresponds to the mystery of life. For most of history, we move along a set path, convinced we understand how the world works. But then, the Control System decides it's time for a shift. It doesn't send a clear memo or scientific manual; instead, it 'kicks the furnace on' by dropping an absurdity into our reality.

Think of a medieval farmer seeing a 'shining wheel' in the sky. He doesn't have the concepts of aerodynamics, so he interprets it as a vision from God. That event changes him and his culture. The 'thermostat' sensed society was ready for a change and provided the spark.

In our modern world, the thermostat stays the same, but it uses different 'outputs' to tamper with our current maps of reality. It doesn't just use metallic discs in the sky traveling at impossible speeds; it uses the shadows of the forest, too. To the 'Control System' a glowing craft over a city and a hairy giant in the woods serve the exact same purpose. They are 'glitches' pushed into our environment.

The brilliance of this process is that it always stays just one step ahead of us. If ET landed on the White House lawn, or if we put a Bigfoot in a zoo, the mystery would be solved. We would put them in a textbook, and the 'thermostat' would have to find another anomaly to influence us.

Instead, the system uses bizarre, dream-like details that make the witnesses look confused, perhaps even a little crazy. By keeping the craft elusive and the forest creatures shadowy, the phenomenon acts like a persistent itch in the back of the human mind. Whether it is a light in the sky or a footprint that leads to nowhere, these events are the clicks and hums of a planetary thermostat. They are slowly 'heating up' the human mind and social evolution.

–Jacques Vallée Control Hypotheses,
White Paper 2026

Alan Megargle

Figure 104: Alan Megargle

Having visited the Church Creek site several times before the summer of 2025, I always sensed something unusual about it, but nothing dramatic. That changed with a series of intriguing investigative experiences.

It started with the REM-POD device triggering, after which the site kept giving and giving. We frequently captured audio anomalies, ranging from Bigfoot images on the FLIR camera, peculiar voice chatter, and wood knocks to infra-sounds and even vocalizations reminiscent of the Sierra sounds.

Although the Church Creek site did not feel as personally significant to me as other locations I've investigated, it possessed a unique sense of vitality. The experiences there seemed to be collective rather than individual, making it thrilling to share what I had witnessed in the past. Recording the voices and vocalizations—just an hour from my home—was remarkable, as it allowed us to play the audio for others and let them hear what we had documented. While the recordings did not match the intensity of the Sierra sounds, they inspired me to continue pursuing further investigations.

With the completion of the film, I look back on an exciting time and memorable summer spent planning and communicating with whatever presence exists at Church Creek. Being able to share these experiences with others has been deeply rewarding.

Ultimately, for me, the appeal lies in chasing the mystery itself. That sense of the unknown is what makes pursuing Bigfoot so much fun. I am no longer searching for definitive answers. Instead, I simply want to experience the phenomenon as it unfolds.

–Alan Megargle, February 2026

Mark Reeder

Figure 105: Mark Reeder

Ron Meyer has been my mentor, teacher, and friend for forty years. We met training at Boulder Aikikai. The Aikido dojo was small back then, with only a few dedicated students training under the watchful eye of Hiroshi Ikeda sensei. Our friendship strengthened over the years and eventually developed into a working relationship with his company Centre Communications. Ron recognized my passion for writing, and for nearly twenty-five years we've worked together on novels, educational videos, and documentaries. In 2021, Ron asked me to help with a book version of his Bigfoot documentary, *The Bigfoot Alien Connection Revealed.*

Ron enlisted my help because, as the preface to the documentary's companion book said: 'Though Mark has experienced several anomalous events in his long life, he remains a paranormal skeptic. Still, the idea of paranormal experiences, like Bigfoot and ET, as emergent forms of religious phenomena, fascinated him, and he agreed.'

The book, *The Bigfoot Alien Connection Revisited,* opened a new and very different world for me, and for the past five years the ensuing work with Ron on his paranormal investigations has greatly changed my life. Most importantly, working with Ron has shown me that being wedded to my skepticism did not allow me to acknowledge that other points of view could be equally as important and valid as my own.

So, when Ron asked me to help with *The High Strangeness of Bigfoot,* he explained that he needed me to write the historical parts that provided evidence of Jacques Vallée's hypothesis. I jumped at the chance, eager to perform my usual historical research but with something more than simply a historian's eye for sifting fact from myth. I would be providing information that could not have been covered in the film owing to time constraints. Jacques Vallée's Control System hypothesis of a presence subtly guiding humanity's development provided a new and oblique understanding of factual events that have shaped humankind over the last 50,000 years.

Historian Carl Becker once complained that 'everybody knows the job of the historian is to discover and set forth the facts of history. The facts, it is said, often speak for themselves.'[1]

So it is true with human history. The facts, on the surface, speak for themselves. Indeed, *The High Strangeness of Bigfoot* is replete with many historical facts. Fact: only humans have a language. Fact: only humans use and create technology. Fact: only humans compose stories about themselves and others. These facts are indisputable. Though *The High Strangeness of Bigfoot* is filled with historical information, scientific investigation and results, the book proposes something greater than the sum of its facts. This volume presents something fresh and new because Ron Meyer's team has stepped beyond the confines of fact and scientific rigor to look at the underlying cause of humanity's rise through the animal kingdom to our present day place at the top. In doing so they have looked at the why of the underlying drama beneath our rise to prominence on this planet.

I must confess that I feel very fortunate to help chronicle Ron and his team's journey in *The High Strangeness of Bigfoot*, for I have come away with a new appreciation for the human condition.

Though it may sound as if Jacques Vallée is saying humans have had no free will for thousands of years, curiously, I do not think of myself or any other person alive today as a pawn in whatever scheme the presence has in store for us. Free will is not binary; it is a spectrum. To that end, we as a species and as individuals have the ability to opt in or out at any time. If we humans are part of a grand design as Vallée proposes, then I am eager to find the intention behind that plan, and I thank Ron for the opportunity to be aware of this possibility.

–Mark Reeder, February 2026

---

1. Lacy Baldwin Smith, Northwestern University, 1970. The Making of England by C. Warren Hollister.

Ronald C. Meyer

Figure 106: Ron Meyer

There were two important takeaways for me. The first came when I conceived of what we call in the book 'The Grand Experiment'—an attempt to provide evidence for Jacques Vallée's control hypothesis. I had serious doubts that anything significant would occur. What did occur exceeded my wildest dreams. My role in the experiment was to keep the whole process moving forward and at the same time gather enough film material to make a movie. Usually this separates me from many of the dramatic occurrences for other people. But this time I did not escape as I heard my name called loud and clear from a disembodied voice. The hearing of the voice was shared by other participants so I could not dismiss it as a mental illusion.

Then again, when we moved to Mount Shasta, I once more had doubts, particularly as the weather seemed to confound us at every step. But when we arrived at Ascension Rock, the presence "spoke again" as a series of Raven caws emphasized the gateway between our ordinary physical life and the nonphysical realm. That was just what Mount Shasta has always been about.

The second and even more profound takeaway for me was that the presence was saying, "look at the origin of language and its autoregressive architecture." It started with rhythmic sounds, each beat following the next, and this pointed to music, which undoubtedly preceded natural language and then protolanguage itself.

At the time only Mark Reeder knew that I was deeply engaged in the autoregressive architecture of Large Language Models and the growing recognition that the autoregressive architecture forms the basis of human language. During that same period we were writing a science fiction novel called Convergence, which is a cautionary tale about how these Large Language Models would eventually evolve into a totally malevolent force controlling all of humanity.

As we chronicled throughout this book, we have shown how humans acquiring natural language marked the separation of humanity from all other biological entities, and how Vallée's proposed idea of an ancient presence moved humans forward by keeping the mystery alive in every domain—from music, the arts, and spirituality to science and particularly technology—all rooted in the autoregressive nature of language.

Finally, I found a hypothesis that linked all anomalous phenomena into one grand picture.

However, although the Raven caw pointed to the connection between our ordinary physical realm and the nonphysical realm, it remains unclear to me if the nonphysical realm is untouched by the ancient presence. The paradox is that the biggest mystery of all is who and what am I beyond the ordinary human ego.

–Ronald C. Meyer, February 2026

Other Books by Ronald C. Meyer and Mark Reeder

Tricksters and Angels

Jesus Had a Near-Death Experience

Aliens 2035: The End of Technology

The Bigfoot Alien Connection Revisited

The High Strangeness of Bradshaw Ranch

Other Books By Mark Reeder

Astral: A Jack Doyle Paranormal Mystery

AFTERWORD

Go to hangar1publishing.com to learn more about the authors and stay up to date with their newest releases.